The Struggle of Two Natures

Me VS Me

Asheley Barnes

letthepaperspeak.com

The Struggle of Two Natures: *Me vs Me*

Copyright © 2022 Asheley Barnes

All rights reserved. Printed in the United States of America.

No part of this book may be used or reproduced in any manner whatsoever without written permission except in the case of brief quotations embodied in critical articles or reviews.

Unless otherwise indicated, all Scripture quotations are from The King James Bible. Scripture quotations marked (ESV) are from The ESV® Bible (The Holy Bible, English Standard Version®), copyright © 2001 by Crossway, a publishing ministry of Good News Publishers. Used by permission. All rights reserved.

The author has tried to recreate personal events, locales, and conversations that evolved from her past.

This book is not intended as a substitute for clinical or spiritual professional counseling. It should not be treated as such.

For information contact:
Asheley Barnes, AuthorAsheley@gmail.com

Developmental Writing Coach & Self-Publishing Consultant:
Sinyon Ducksworth, letthepaperspeak.com
Cover Designer: Brandon Jolly, www.brangraphicd.com
Author Photos: Ta'Mekia Baker

ISBN: 9798846567009

First Edition: August 2022

Dedication

I dedicate this book back to the one who blessed me with the gift to write because without him, none of this would have been possible. With the help of the Holy Spirit, I was able to share with you the things the Spirit gave to me.

Thank you, Jesus, for everything. Every trial and victory that I had to endure. Many times, I wanted to give up and at times, I did not obey you. But you never left me

With gratitude, Thank you!

(1 Peter 4:10-11, ESV)

"As each has received a gift, use it to serve one another as good stewards of God's varied grace: whoever speaks, as one who speaks oracles of God; whoever serves, as one who serves by the strength that God supplies- in order that in everything God may be glorified through Jesus Christ. To him belongs glory and dominion forever and ever. Amen."

Part I

~

Before the Storm

ACTS 4:12 (ESV)

And there is salvation in no one else, for there is no other name under heaven given among men by which we must be saved.

Romans 10:9 (KJV)

That if thou shalt confess with thy mouth the Lord Jesus, and shalt believe in thine heart that God hath raised him from the dead, thou shalt be saved.

Chapter 1

"My Gentle Giant"

My life struggles started on August 07, 2007, with the passing of my little brother. He died at the age of seventeen due to a heat stroke playing football. After his death, I began to question God about why he took him at such a young age.

"Why didn't you take me instead?" I cried out.

The life I knew was over. For 18 years, Lonnie had always been there with me. My emotions were all over the place, I started feeling guilty for all the times we fought, and smiled at the times when we would get on our older sister's nerves. We talked about how we would travel the world. He wanted to be a football player but was also interested in building cars, and how he wanted to get our mom a house built. God we were still in high school, this was our senior year and he was not there (I have tears in my eyes now just thinking about it). It was a tough time not just for me but for my family as well. He was truly our "Gentle Giant". He got that name because he was big in stature but his heart was genuine. I just could not understand why God needed him so badly when we needed him more. I was so angry and hurt for a long time that I blamed myself for my brother's death. He needed a signed physical to play football. That morning before we got onto the bus, he left the paper on the table, and I ran back into the house to get it for him.

That seemingly insignificant moment became all I thought about. I turned that moment over and over again in my mind. If I would have known it would be the last time I would see my brother again, I would have left that paper on the table. I should have left that paper on the table. The fear of no one understanding the level of pain I was experiencing made it easy for me to hold everything in. I didn't want to talk about how I was feeling nor did I show any emotions. I bottled them and pushed them to the back of my mind thinking of ways to handle the fact that my little brother is no longer with us. I had to hide the way I felt so I could be strong for my mom and sister. My family had stated once that I was acting differently, truth is they were right because I didn't know how to express what I was feeling. We all handled this pain according to how we understood it. On top of all this, I still had to face reality and go to school.

I was no longer focused on school. A new year had begun with this dreadful tragedy looming over me, weighing on me, destroying me inside. I wanted to quit so many times, everything reminded me of him. What was supposed to be a senior year full of fun senior activities, was overshadowed by spaces filled with my brother. I could see him jutting down the school hallways, sitting in first period with me, his laughter across the school cafeteria. It was agonizing to be there. So, I went inside myself and almost stopped going altogether. My family and friends encouraged me to stay. So I stayed. But I was a ghost walking through dusty halls, sitting in broken desks, existing but not living. I would lay in bed at night with those thoughts turning in my head. And then unbelief. Overwhelming disbelief that he was actually gone.

REST IN HEAVEN LONNIE C. MAGEE JR

JUNE 13, 1990 - AUGUST 8, 2007

Chapter 2

"I Moved Out"

During the first year of college, some friends and I carpooled. One morning we were on our normal commute. I was the driver for that day because they had other agendas. One of the friends in the back seat told me to roll the windows up, and they hot-boxed the car. Two blunts were in rotation. And they kept smoking until the car was engulfed with smoke. I caught contact high, my eyes were on fire, and everything was in slow motion. It felt funny at first but after a while, I was so calm, as if I was on a dock looking out on the sea. It was a soothing after-effect. Once we made it to school, we opened the doors and it was like the car was on fire. It was an experience I will never forget. After that day, I wanted to hot box all the time. I wanted that feeling again and again. I would smoke before school and after. Smoking became an escape route for me to deal with grief.

At the end of that year, I met up with my friends and we all went out to a New Year's Eve house party that was down the street from my mom's house. They knew I was not myself after everything with my brother so they got me out of the house. It was my first time out without my brother tagging along. After a few drinks and smoking, I was able to take my mind off things at least until after I slept it off. After that night, going out became an every weekend kind of thing. My mom did not like who I was becoming. We had a disagreement because of the late nights so I decided to leave her house. I moved in with a friend and that's when most of my family felt as if I had lost my mind. None of them knew that this was how I was dealing with losing my Lonnie.

I started dancing at this club at night and worked a full-time job during the day. I was so caught up with the fast money and doing things on my own I didn't realize how concerned my mom was about me. All I cared about was being free to do what I wanted, indulge in what I wanted, escaping. I felt grown no longer living under her roof. But I did not know what life was about until I got out there in it. I lived with this friend for about a year until it was a misunderstanding that caused me to leave her house and I moved in with a coworker. I stayed with a co-worker for about six months. And when things had cooled down at my friend's house, I moved back in with her. I stopped dancing but I was still smoking and drinking plenty.

By this time, I had so many bad experiences with dating men that I decided it was time to try something different. I was at a point in my life where I was trying to figure out who I was. I dated a girl for a few months but it still did not make me happy. So, that relationship didn't last long. I found out that dating a female was almost the same as dating a male. There were still lies, hurt feelings, and arguing so I was better off alone. At this point, I had given up on love and relationships. I decided it was best if I just try to live my life to the fullest and live for my brother because he did have a chance to. I thought I could live for us both. Gosh, I missed him so much. Why I was still here baffled me. But, I didn't understand the will nor the plans God had. And I didn't know who God really was.

Chapter 3

"When We Met"

One Saturday my friend was getting ready to go out. As I sat on her bed rolling a blunt, watching her do her makeup, out of nowhere she asked, "Do you want to go to church tomorrow?"

I was lost for words. I looked at her like she had asked me to kill someone!

"Go to church?" I asked.

"Yes. To church with me tomorrow."

With a confused look on my face, I lit the blunt, pulled on it, blew smoke out, and said, "Sure why not?" All while thinking to myself it's the liquor talking. She cannot be serious.

We went out, had fun and came back home. The next morning, sure enough, she walked into the room I was sleeping in and asked, "You going to church?"

With sleep in my eyes and feeling everything I had done the night before, I said, "So you were serious about going to church?"

"Yes!" my friend persisted.

I shook my head, pulled myself together, and got dressed. We pulled into the church parking lot, and I instantly started sweating. I was so nervous, I didn't know what to expect. I had on pants with a shirt and boots. In the church I attended as a child, you could not wear pants. So I was thinking, *these people about to say something to me, and I know I am going to say something back.*

I was that person who didn't care who you were or where I was. I was not tolerating disrespect from anyone. But when we walked into the church, shocking to me, no one said anything. At least not to me directly. There were strange looks, but no confrontations. The church service was actually good, even though I did not understand anything the preacher said. That same evening after church I was sitting outside the house in the back of an old car smoking (as you can see, I was a heavy smoker). It was like I was having a conversation with myself in my head. I was replaying something I had heard during the sermon. I have never been to a church service and come home and still remember what was said, nor did I know that the Spirit of God works that way.

I got out of the car and walk inside to ask my friend when we were going back to church. She looked at me and started laughing. I was high so I started laughing too but I was serious! I heard that the pastor of my friend's church was preaching at a local church during a revival, so I went. That night I was so captivated by what I was listening to, it was like he was talking directly to me as if someone had given him personal information about me. I wanted to know more about what he was talking about because I never heard it that way before. I started going to church regularly. I wanted to join but I was still a member at my old church and wasn't sure if it was the right move. So, I waited it out until the time was right.

The following Sunday I walked to the altar just for prayer, I told myself. I wanted so badly to be saved and join the church, but I said nothing because I knew what I was about to do when I left church. I was not ready to give all that up yet. Prayer would have to be enough for now. After church that Sunday, I was standing in the parking lot and this guy caught my eye. I was looking at him, he was looking at me. Then I turned my head as if I was not staring. I turned to my friend's daughter and asked, "Who's the guy with the dreads?"

She was like, "That's my cousin, Chip."

"Oh, okay. He fine. I know I am coming back to church next Sunday." I teased.

We both laughed. But I was contemplating as we got in the car to leave. All that week, I could not get this guy out of my head. All I could see were those beautiful locks flowing from his crown and that cute smile. I searched social media and could not find him anywhere, not dawning on me that Chip was his nickname. I had another objective for going to that church. I wanted to meet Chip. And the next Sunday, I got my chance. He walked over and introduced himself. We exchanged numbers. I had recently gotten a tattoo of a gang-related symbol on my hand. He asked me what it was. I told him the correlation of it to my family's set. His energy shifted. He looked at me and said, "I don't talk to rough girls. Thug girls."

I stared at him for a moment confused. Weren't we all a little rough?

He clarified, "I don't talk to G-Queens."

Then it hit me. He had to be from the opposite set. But I desired to get to know more about him. So, I pivoted. "Oh no. This tat was a bet and I lost." I concealed the fact that I was planning to become a G-Queen. And I wasn't sure how talking to him would affect my chances. He seemed to be cool with my response for the moment. Later, I called a cousin and asked him if it was against the rules to date outside the set. He simply said as long as it's no disrespect. But I never got initiated so it didn't matter to me. Little did I know, it would matter to others.

Chapter 4

"Something Happened"

I had been attending church for some time now and like before, the service was mind-blowing. But this one particular Sunday, something happened that changed my life completely. I was sitting in the pew, mind full of pain and hurt. Thinking about all the things that were wrong in my life. How I kept going in circles and how my life was just not right. Listening to the preacher talk about a man who carried the sins of the world to the dirt. I did not understand all that he was saying, but I listened anyway. Thinking to myself–*Who is this man? How can he take my pain away?*

The preacher continued to tell Jesus's story, His death, burial, and resurrection. How His blood covered all sin and life without Him was no life; this fight I could not win. He talked about how his death gave me life more abundantly. But with my carnal eyes, I couldn't see it happening.

The only thing I could think about was–*This man did what? For who? And he did this why?*

As the preacher finished the sermon, I saw people jumping and shouting, raising their hands, and crying. And I was sitting there like, *what is going on in here?* In my head, someone just died, got hung on a cross, and was beaten. *And they are happy about this?*

I had zero understanding of our savior. *Then they put him in the grave and somehow, he got up?* I was shocked and confused about what was going on.

While sitting there with my mind cloudy and trying to process what I just heard, over all the noise I heard a voice.

Give me your life!

Then I heard the preacher say, "Who wants to make Jesus their personal savior?"

Before I knew it my hands were in the air, palms sweating, heart beating fast, tears flowing down my face, and I had no clue why all of this was happening. But I knew something was going on inside of me. For the first time, my spirit was happy.

All the while, I was wondering if I walked to that altar would this man conquer my fears, could he wipe away all my tears?

As I got closer to the altar the preacher looked at me and said, "Do you believe that God has a son named Jesus?"

"Yes," I replied.

He continued with the rest but it was a blur because, at that moment, I was crying harder. And my hands were lifted higher. And I still did not know what was happening.

I had this unexplainable feeling going on inside like my soul was on fire. The next thing I knew, I was on the floor on my knees, arms raised high thanking God for what had happened. I did not understand what it was, but I knew that something on the inside of me had woken up! With a loud cry and tears falling uncontrollably, I knew at that moment that God had a purpose for my life that I could not see.

This was a new beginning, the transition from the old to the new me. Free from all sin and that I was no longer going to sin after this. At least this is what I was thinking. I believed that the devil was finally off my track, not knowing I just put a target on my back. I was happy anyway because of the salvation I had just received. I can truly say that day was life-changing for me, something did happen. I went from being an enemy to God to a friend of His.

After that day I still did not understand what was about to happen, or what I would do now after being saved. All I was thinking was that I am saved, now things will be easy. I had a lot to learn it was so much more. My journey was just beginning. Going to church services, Bible classes, and classes were excellent ways I got my questions answered. It also helped me understand more of what salvation was, and why it was important for Jesus to die on the cross for humanity. I was on fire for the Lord, but deep down I still had issues that needed to be addressed.

Journal entry - *Salvation scriptures for meditation*

(Romans 6:23a, KJV)
"Sin separated us from GOD, and the consequences or the wage of sin is death."

(Titus 3:5, KJV)
"Salvation is our deliverance from sin, the consequences of sin, and from eternal punishment for sin. Only GOD can remove sin and deliver us from sin's penalty, which cannot be accomplished by our works, but according to his mercy."

(Romans 5:10b, KJV).
"We are salvaged (preserved and rescued) through Jesus' death on the cross and the resurrection that achieved our salvation."

(Ephesians 2:8-9, KJV)

"Salvation is a grace gift from GOD it is only available through faith in Jesus Christ"

(2 Corinthians 5:17, KJV)

"When salvation impacts our spirit, our sins are forgiven, our guilt and shame is removed, and our place in eternity is secured. It is at salvation that we become new creatures; old things pass away, and behold all things are new"

Food for Thought:

Once we have received salvation, God offers us forgiveness. We know and understand that God has forgiven our past, present, and future sins through His son Jesus. The part that keeps us stuck is forgiving ourselves…

Chapter 5

"Chip Moved In"

It was a few months after I had given my life to Christ when Chip moved in with me and my mom. My life had calmed down a great deal and my Mom's place was home again. With Chip there, things started great. We talked about what we wanted in life, and past relationships. We shared secrets no one else knew about us. I could finally say I had found love. But after some time passed, I started seeing another side of Chip. I knew he drank alcohol, but I didn't know the level of it or his reaction to it until one devastating night.

I was working at a convenience store and my shift was over. I didn't have a vehicle at the time, so I was waiting for a ride. I called Chip to let him know that I was off and that I'd be home shortly. Well, my cousin came to pick me up and she made a stop before we came straight home. Chip called wondering what was taking me so long. I told him my cousin made a stop. I did have a history of talking with many guys before him. No commitments, just having my fun. A few of my past entertainment had run-ins with Chip during the beginning of our dating phase while I was still purging myself from them. So, I understood why he had concerns. What I didn't know was how concerns could escalate into full paranoia for someone with a drinking problem. And I discovered he had a serious problem.

I had finally made it home. While I was walking through the door, things immediately got out of control. The side of Chip I was witnessing shook me. We had been dating for three months, and this was the first time he erupted in such a way. He was so angry and was hurling accusations at me: "I know that it was some guy who dropped you off! You must think I am stupid or something?"

I was trying to explain but there was nothing I could have said or done to calm him down. I would find out later that my family had played a prank on him and he was not used to their kind of humor. It all had built up and was exploding in my face. I was afraid because I never had to deal with anything like this before. I had gone to sit in my closet to shelter myself from his rantings. *Did I make a mistake to let this man live with me and my mom? What if he kills me in my sleep?* Bizarre thoughts began running in my head as my anxiety level rose. For the rest of that night, I sat and thought and was afraid to sleep. The next day, Chip was back to the guy I met. I was relieved. We talked and I explained to him what had happened. He apologized, and things seemed to be okay again.

Six months later, we were still going to church and the knowledge he had about the word of God was amazing to me. He inspired me to read and study more about God's word. We had deep discussions about the word and my mom was eager to join our conversations. My mom loved Chip when he was not too intoxicated. And honestly, I felt that way too. I felt he really could be the one if only he could get the drinking under control.

One Sunday night we all had just finished dinner. I told my mom goodnight before Chip and I went to bed. I was tired but wanted to finish some laundry before going to sleep. He was laying across the bed and I was folding our clothes. Chip looked up at me and asked if would I marry him. I thought he was playing because that's not how I pictured my future husband asking for my hand in marriage. I didn't say anything because at that time I was not in love with him. The strong feelings for him were there. But, I was not ready for that.

He asked again. "Will you marry me?"

Something on the inside said, *Girl, said no*. Another part of me wanted to say yes. That's what came out. Yes.

Then I asked, "You sure this is what you want?" We had only been dating for nine months at this time, but he seemed sure. He told me that he was in love with me. I really couldn't see how when it had been a short time for me. And we were just fussing the day before. I was confused about his motives and what I wanted. Honestly, I did not know what I was saying when I agreed. I was twenty-two years old and had not experienced life the way I wanted to experience it. I had not experienced traveling out of the country. I had not even ventured out of Mississippi! And now I was engaged? Wow, this was moving way too fast! But I did not know how to pump the brakes. Although I was apprehensive about all of it, a part of me was still excited to be marrying him. Sounds crazy, but this is where I was. Torn between two desires. Conflicted versions of myself fighting to speak. The struggle of two natures.

Chapter 6

"Oil & Vinegar"

I had already met Chip's family and they were such amazing people, showing me so much love. But they had a lot of questions. I didn't mind, figuring that it was just to get to know me better. Chip's relationship with my family was strained. It pained me that his welcome into my family was not as warm as what his family had given me. Chip was an introvert. Some of my family members had an issue with him because of that. My family lived next door to one another and loved to hang out and commune together. They had a certain way of doing and living amongst each other. Chip, an outsider in more ways than one, did not seem to fit their liking. It was unnatural to them that Chip isolated himself from their gatherings. While I was at work, he would sit in the house until I got off. He could not understand why it mattered to them so much what he did with his time. It went from being a problem that he stayed in the house all the time, to an issue of sharing food. Next, it was cutting grass. All these things may have been petty, but they were a real issue for my family members. With everyone staying in their place, my family ran like a well-oiled machine. And Chip was vinegar.

One night things came to a head. It was August 2012. There was a storm coming and one of my family members came to the house to let us know that they had put their dog outside to keep watch. Chip came to the door as well just to see what was going on. He had been drinking. My family member decided to have some words with Chip about everything that was going on and the conversation got heated. I was trying to calm both of them down but neither would listen. I grabbed Chip and kind of pushed him to the back of the house. But the family member insisted on carrying on the dispute.

"Can we talk about this some other time," I pleaded? "This is not the right time for all this nonsense!"

I felt in such an awkward position. I had my family who understood everything I had gone through and then my guy I cared about deeply, both at each other's throats about something irrelevant. I was being pulled in different directions. What was I supposed to do?

I remember Chip putting his foot down. "I am here for only Asheley and her mom. If I don't want to talk to anyone about my choices, that's my business. I am going to be with Asheley and I don't care who likes or dislikes it!"

I was shocked because no one I have dated ever stood up to this family member like that. And at that point, I knew I was dealing with a man that was not afraid to speak his mind. I liked it. After that, the family member left. Chip was still mad and it took another hour to calm down enough to have a decent conversation. We talked, and I told him I knew how this family member operates and that we should be thinking of somewhere to move. I was right. The next day, Chip was asked to leave my mom's house or the police would be called. My mom knew that my family wanted Chip gone long before. But I felt that she had been trying to avoid the issue because she liked Chip, and I had just moved back with her. She didn't want to lose me again.

I asked my mom what she wanted. "This is your house and no one can just tell you to put someone out of your house." I waited for a response but I realized I didn't need it. I could see in my mom's eyes that she was so hurt. I knew the answer. She just cried. But I was furious. I wanted to just walk across the street and yell at everyone because the whole situation was insane. I called a close friend of mine and asked him to hang out with Chip until I got off work. I told Chip we would figure something out later that night. My friend was okay with it because he and Chip had hung out before. I packed our stuff and we loaded them into my friend's car.

I looked into my mom's pained face. "I love you. But if you can't speak up for us, then I have to go too."

Then we left.

Chapter 7

"For Better, Not Worse"

My shift at work had started but my mind kept replaying everything that had happened. I kept thinking about where we were going to go. I was the only one working and I didn't have enough money for a hotel room. I was checking a customer out and Chip came bursting through the front door out of nowhere. I could tell that he was drunk. My heart started racing because I knew this was not going to be good. With everything he had been through on top of what just happened earlier that day, drinking was his way of dealing with the difficulty of it all.

Chip started ranting loudly. "You need to leave! We got to go!"

I quickly finished checking out the customer. "I can't just leave. There is no one to take my spot!" I tried explaining.

But he insisted. I asked where my friend was. He was sitting in the car. I asked the lady I was working with to allow me to step outside for a moment. I walked outside to talk to my friend because Chip was not making any sense.

"Why did you bring him back up here like that?" I asked my friend.

"He wanted to see you," he shrugged.

No matter how I tried to calm him, Chip was not taking no for an answer. So, that evening I quit my job. Now I was homeless and jobless with no clue about what to do at this point. Going to his family was out of the question. Returning to mine was a no. I had no one. I had so many mixed emotions going on. I thought about just leaving him and going back home alone. I wanted to cry, scream. Everything but pray.

Outside looking in at myself, I am like, "Girl why you just didn't let him go? All the signs were there to leave him where he was!" And I want to agree. Yet, there was something in me that felt that's where I needed to be and for some odd reason, I felt I could change him.

So there we were, riding nowhere in my friend's car. Trying to figure out what we were about to do. Chip blurted out, "Take us to another city."

I looked at my friend and he looked at me. "Do what?" I said.

"I have a cousin that will let us stay. So, take us to his city," Chip insisted.

We had nothing else to lose. I handed my friend thirty dollars, all I had left for gas. He agreed to take us but wouldn't take my money. Once we got to the city, things took a turn. The cousin didn't know we were coming. We had no money. We had no plans. But Chip was right. His cousin would help. We lived with his cousin for a few months then we got our own apartment. This is where life forced me to grow up and stand on my own.

It was November 2012 and we were settling into our new place. Life had started to settle into somewhat of a comfortable rhythm and we were happy for the most part. Then the marriage conversations started again. You'd think any agreeable feelings I had previously about marrying this man would have since ceased after the hell we went through. But no, I still was willing to marry him. So on December 12, 2012, we got married at his mom's house during his family's annual Christmas party. I remember one of his sisters was doing my makeup and there were other family members of his in the room as well. They took the opportunity to present me with another round of questioning. This time it was about Chip. They asked me if was I sure this was what I wanted. His family knew he was a lot to handle so they were just checking to make sure I knew what I was getting myself into. Still not knowing myself and the fullness of this man, or what marriage would entail for us, I gave them a reassured yes. I had no idea what marriage was supposed to be like, nor did I know how hard it was going to be. Somehow I thought whatever it was, it would make things different for the better not worse.

Chapter 8

"A Long Winter"

The married life I had while living in our new city consisted of a lot of arguing, fighting, and breaking things. We both threatened divorce. The first four years of our marriage were unbearable. Chip's drinking got worse. I left him numerous times and came back. I felt so alone out in the cold of a long winter. The city was not kind to me. I felt everything was on my shoulders. The name-calling between us, at times Chip made me feel like I didn't belong in this world. I questioned my decisions daily, asking myself why I let this man come into my life and destroy my self-confidence. He made me feel so low as if I could not do better. I stayed emotionally disturbed. I wanted to talk to family members about what I was dealing with but I knew all they would say is: *you knew how he was before you married him,* or *only you can change what you're going through.* I remember that one time I was told, "Don't call me anymore if you're just going to keep talking about it and do nothing about it."

All of this made me realize that I was alone in this. Going to church was not something we wanted to do anymore. We caught rides back home to attend our church in the beginning but then it was like life pulled me in too deep to recognize that God was still there. I started to search for a church that was close to where we lived. Nothing seemed to work. I started to smoke marijuana again, just to sleep at first. It was not something I enjoyed doing. It was something I needed to deal with the struggles of being married to this person I didn't recognize and the chaotic life I had created for myself.

January 2013 came. I got a job working at a local hospital as a housekeeper. Still no vehicle. So, I walked to work every morning, catching a ride with a coworker on the way home each evening. Chip did walk with me to work. Even though we had our issues, I knew deep down past all the hidden struggles he had that he loved me. I guess that's what kept me fighting so hard. I worked at the hospital for almost two years. During that time, our marriage troubles grew worse instead of better. I kept losing sleep after working ten hours a day. Some days walking home, then get there and argue because I don't have enough money to pay bills and support his habits at the same time. Just writing this brings tears to my eyes because I didn't recognize it then, but

God had his hands around me. Keeping me. And still today, He keeps me.

"Thank you, Lord!"

Part II

~

During The Storm

"On This Journey"

The way things were going it just wasn't right, I figured I had lost sight.

Things were falling down around me, I didn't know what to do, and then I remembered that I had a friend in you.

Tried to do things myself, and that never seemed to work out, then I realized that trusting in your word was what it's all about.

I never lost my faith in you, nor did yours in me, I'm on this journey of life striving to be who you called me to be.

I hurt a lot of people including me along the way, restore back to me the joy of my salvation, is the prayer I pray.

You love me so, Jesus, and I've failed you so many times, that's how I know your love is true, holy, and divine. You give chance after chance even when we don't deserve it, I believe faith comes by hearing and I truly believe in your word.

Lord renew my mind, and keep me in perfect peace, as I'm working on myself on this journey.

A Poem By: Lee O. Barnes Jr. (Chip)

Chapter 9

"Where is Chip?"

One night Chip had gone out with his cousin, and I was home alone which was beginning to be a normal thing. This time, Chip didn't come home. It was three o'clock in the morning and I was calling everyone that he was with to see where Chip was. No one knew where he was.

I snapped! "How you lose a human being!"

Their only explanation was, "we looked for him all night."

I called Chip's phone. No answer. I looked at the time and it was now six a.m. I had to be at work in an hour. No sleep. Panic in overdrive, I was shaking uncontrollably. I didn't know what to think. *Was he dead? Did something happen to him?* For all I knew, he could've been with a woman. And his boys were covering for him! My mind was everywhere.

I jumped in the shower and just stood there with hot water running down on me as I cried. I did not realize it was all hot water! I couldn't feel a thing. I was numb from the inside out. At some point, I must have gotten out because I remembered being dressed for work. Then, walking to the lady's house across the street to catch a ride. Tears streamed down my face. I continued calling the cousins asking if they heard anything. Calling Chip's phone. Still, no answer. We pulled into the parking lot at work, and I just sat there. The lady asked if I wanted to talk and if I was okay. I just nodded, *yes*. I asked her for a cigarette. It was my first time. And it became another habit.

I crossed the street to walk into the hospital entrance for housekeepers when my phone rang. It was a man with an unfamiliar voice.

"Who is this?" I asked.

"Umm. I found this phone in my truck next to a man that's sleeping–in my truck."

My legs got weak. My heart raced. I fought back fresh tears. "Can you wake him up?" my voice quivered. "But do it gently because if he does not recognize where he is it could alarm him."

I hear the guy trying to wake Chip up. After three attempts, I hear Chip. He gets on the phone. "Baby, I don't know where I am!" he sounds hungover. "Can you come get me?"

"How the hell I'm gonna come get you, Chip! And you don't even know where you are neither? How you think

I know? And we don't have a ride, remember!" I must admit, I was happy and mad.

I had called my friend and asked if she could ride the street he was on that night to see if she saw him. The guy got back on the phone and gave me the address. So, I texted it to my friend. Then, I took a deep, composed myself, and walked into work. All that day, my thoughts were all over the place. My anxiety levels stayed on ten.

There are so many situations like this that have transpired over the years. So many sleepless nights. Me crying myself to sleep or just being an emotional wreck. During all this, never did it cross my mind to fall on my face and cry out to God. The only one who could have given me the strength to endure all of this. My marriage was not a marriage at all. I felt as if I was married to myself. I felt that he didn't care enough to see how bad I was hurting. There were so many times I wanted to just talk with him, but the talks always ended in a fight. So, I eventually shut down and held it all in.

There are some good memories and times we shared. I can recall a time during Valentine's Day. I remember it was our first one together after being married. With no job, I knew Chip had no money to go all out for me. So, I didn't expect much. I had gotten off work, and when I walked into the house, I was in total shock! Chip had run my bath water and cooked for me *(I have to say, he cooks for me all the time. I love that about him)*. He had a card in his hand. I got out of the tub and he handed the card to me and it was the most thoughtful thing he had done. He handmade the card and it was beautiful! It meant a lot to me because he took out time to make this. I read the card and it made me cry.

I also remember thinking, *"why can't you be this guy every day?"*

I told him from that day forward that's how I wanted all my cards to be. So for birthdays, anniversaries, and other holidays, I always get a thoughtful handmade card. No, every day was not heartwrenching. We've had awesome date nights, and moments of intimacy just being in each other's company. There were days when he was such a lovable person to be around, I didn't want to be anywhere else.

Chapter 10

"Where is Asheley?"

Somewhere in the hurt and mixed emotions, I lost who I was. I had changed to please him. A man that at moments didn't seem to care if I was dead or alive. Drinking was consuming him. It became more important than fixing a broken marriage. Honestly, neither of us understood what it took to make it work because we had eliminated the main source, God.

People at work worried about me. Around this time I had a select few that I could trust to talk to. My supervisor called me into the office one day to tell me that my work performance was low. The rating number on my floor went from one hundred to eighty percent, which was not good. He asked why the sudden change. I just responded that I had a lot going on and I will try to do better. My supervisor was a close friend to my husband, so that made me feel as if I could trust him with opening up about what I was dealing with. He knew Chip's ways, so it wasn't like I was divulging our business out for any and everybody to gossip about, I reasoned with myself. I started to talk to him about what was going on. He gave me encouraging words to hang in there and try to separate my personal life from my work life. I did.

In 2015, things with Chip and I got a little better. He had a job and we were no longer living in the apartments. We were renting a house. I quit my hospital job and got a less demanding fast-food gig so I could finally get back in school. I felt that things were getting on track because we were out of our previous environment which caused so much drama. Chip had even made more efforts to stop picking fights with me. But he still was drinking. But I was numb to it by now. I came to grips that this was who he was and this is the life I had chosen. So I had to deal with it the best way I knew how. Tucking parts of me inside myself was one of the ways I coped. Finding secret warmth outside my marriage was another. Still turning to external comforts, I didn't think to seek solace and intimacy in God.

Neither one of us knew what the future held but we kept trying. I knew that Chip had to battle his demons and drinking was a way for him to deal with them. I can't just keep pointing out all his flaws. I had some demons too. One was harboring suppressed guilt I had cheated on him. I was mentally broken, my anger was out of control, and some days I didn't know if I was going or coming. I worked a lot, so I didn't have to deal with the real issues of my life. I was under so much stress that I began to lose weight without trying. No one knew the deep thoughts in my mind but God. There was a part of me that longed for the spirit of God, but it was unfamiliar to me at this point in my life. I just smoked weed instead. I told myself if I could stay high, I could just float through this marriage unnoticed. I felt like that anyway.

Chapter 11

"Back Home Again"

In 2017, we moved back home and back with my mom. But this time was different. My family and I were on speaking terms again, and they had accepted Chip as family. We started going back to our church where everything first started. It felt so good to be back. I was thinking this was a chance for us to start over and forget about all the things that happened in the other city. Focus on a new beginning. Maybe the experiences I had in that city, and everything my husband and I had to go through were needed. I hadn't realized that before. So, I was determined to give us a go with a renewed mindset of sorts.

We still had some hurdles. The drinking was still there but not as heavy. And the guilt of my unfaithfulness weighed on my soul, on top of all the pain and trauma that had taken up space in my heart. It haunted me. It was heavy, but there was no way I was saying a word. I was well accustomed to the type of man I married. And how he handled letdowns or even the thought of me stepping out.

I had a job the week after we moved back. Chip was waiting to get his old job back. And the *wait* brought some up and down moments, testing our fragile marriage once again. But, I refused to have that mindset again, so I remained focused. Eventually, Chip got a job and the tension eased. We both were working. We both had vehicles. I transitioned to another job in a town nearby. We were doing so well, that we moved out of my mom's house and got our place nearby. It was amazing! We were finally happy. Chip and I talked about our future, and for the first time, I felt like I was married to a man that wanted me, not just needed me. Like truly invested in building a life with me!

We were attending church every Sunday and Bible class. We were on a roll. But our minds still had not been renewed. Our habits were worse than before. I was smoking every day before work, during work, and after work. All day. That little girl that had left that evening from the convenience store back in 2012 was dead. I was someone else entirely. Someone I seriously didn't recognize. Honestly, who I was had altered so much starting way back when I lost my Gentle Giant, it would have exhausted me trying to unravel her. I was done trying to figure it out. I was working with what I had and making the best of it.

All the emotions I had once harbored and the drive to want to fix my husband, and marriage was all dead. I was on autopilot going through life's motions just to get by. I was not living, I was only existing. The pain and hurt from my past, life in the dark city, the passing of my brother, and everything I had been through were all bottled up and locked away in a closet in the back of my mind. There was no way I was opening that door and retrieving that bottle ever again.

I equipped this new me with *don't give a care* buffers to never be hurt again. Neither would she feel like she was nothing again for no one. I was still a broken individual and didn't want to be fixed. But after some time in this new place, I started to see a pattern like I was reliving the same pain all over again. I would be hit with spells of despair that I couldn't even tell you what triggered it and why. Although I didn't want to face my demons, that didn't stop them from gnawing at my insides. You have something making your insides sick long enough, you have no choice but to start seeking a change. So I started looking for relief. I did not know that it had to start with me. I knew that there had to be another way but could not see it.

Chapter 12

"Seeking God Again"

After my husband got his old job back, his old ways came back with it. Not as bad as they were before, but slowly progressed backward. I was working two jobs: at a convenience store and back doing housekeeping at a local hospital. I got back in a good place for a moment. I had rededicated my life back to Christ. I finally felt that fire again that I had been missing for so long. I was reading the word more. And for the first time, instead of going to others, I was going to God. It felt good, no longer turning outside to be comforted. I still knew I had to answer for the times I had. I knew I still had some hidden issues that eventually I had to address, but I was trying to forget all that. But it was like the more I studied the word of God the more the things in the closet wanted to escape.

I still held my husband hostage for the things he put me through. I just couldn't seem to forgive him for that. And I wouldn't let go until I understood what forgiveness was. I had to do a little more soul searching within myself. I went back and started to work on *me* with the help of the Holy Spirit. *What did my salvation really mean? I needed to know.*

Learning about forgiveness, and learning how to forgive was my first step.

Journal Entry - *Notes on Forgiveness*

According to Romans 8:1 (KJV), "there is now no condemnation to those who are in Christ Jesus, who walk not after the flesh but after the spirit. God absolves (set us free) from the condemnation and guilt of sin. Thus, pardoning man from the guilt and penalty of sin."

(Colossians 1:27, KJV)
"We are translated from the Kingdom of darkness to the Kingdom of His son, wherein we have redemption, the forgiveness of sins".

Thought - God has forgiven the iniquity of man through his son Jesus.

Forgiveness means to wipe the slate clean, to pardon, to cancel a debt. The only just penalty for our sins is death. Eternal death is what we have earned for our sins. However,

Jesus took the punishment for our sins that we deserved on the cross. His death provided forgiveness of sin.

(Read Isaiah 38:17)
God is a holy, righteous God, but He is willing to forgive.

(Read Luke 15:11-32)
He is like the father in the parable of the prodigal son: instead of giving the son what he deserved and not receiving him, or even just keeping him as a slave, the father lovingly restores his son to the bosom of the family.

(Hebrews 10:17a, KJV)
"He does not even remember the wrongs committed, "Their sins and lawless deeds I will remember no more."

It does not matter if you are young or old, tall, or short, male or female if you have money or you're broke. What you have done to people, or what people have done to you, it does not matter. We all need forgiveness, and we receive it through the blood of Jesus and Him alone.

(ACTS 10:43b, ESV)
"That everyone who believes in Him receives forgiveness of sins through His name."

Knowing that we were forgiven by the grace of God through Christ Jesus was an outstanding revelation for me. Once I understood that Jesus had done more for me than I could have done for myself, I began to view situations (life) differently. Jesus took the penalty for the world's sins when they nailed Him to the cross (that was supposed to have been me dying for my own sins). Seeing this made it easier for me to forgive my husband, and to look beyond his faults.

I sat and thought about all the times I had done stupid things, with the mindset I had, living for God was not on the agenda at all. I was comfortable living in sin because it was a familiar area of my life and I thought I knew what was best for me. But I was realizing all I did was create a problem or make the problems worse.

Chapter 13

"The Burdens We Carry"

After getting saved years back, it seemed as if life itself had gotten harder to deal with. I did not realize there was more conversion that needed to take place in my life, like transforming my mind to be more like Christ. Even after obtaining knowledge of our Savior, I still chose to do what I wanted. In the midst of me doing what I wanted, God never left me alone. He was still there waiting on me and ready to forgive me. I am so grateful for His mercy and amazing grace! I should not be here sharing all the things I had gotten myself into, but he still provided a way out for me. The fact that God knew I was going to be hard-headed, and He still had a master plan to forgive me and give me chances after chances to surrender completely to Him. Without the blood of Jesus and if I had to face God on my behalf, I realized my penalty would have been death due to sin. Not just the sin I partake in but also the sins I was born into. Thank you, Jesus, for loving us enough to take our judgment.

Journal entry - *Christ sets us free meditation*

(Ephesians 2:1, ESV)

"And you were dead in the trespasses and sins."

(Ephesians 2:5, ESV)

"Even when we were dead in our trespasses, made us alive together with Christ – by grace you have been saved."

(Acts 13:38-39, ESV)

"Let it be known to you therefore, brothers, that through this man forgiveness of sins is proclaimed to you, and by him everyone who believes is freed from everything from which you could not be freed by the Law of Moses."

I forgave Chip and decided to move on from the hurt. It was not completely gone once I chose to forgive. I still had an ache in my heart. But I chose with the understanding of what Christ had done for me. It made it easier to deal with the things I could see and trust God for the things I could not see. I slowly began enjoying my husband more and our times together, once I stopped looking at his faults. And then the clouds turned dark again. And more storms rolled in.

Chip lost his job due to his drinking. It felt like daggers. Everything I was learning was lost with it. I tried not to hold him in contempt for it at first, but as time progressed, I started to feel the pressure. In the back of my mind, all I could think was, *here we go again.* I started working at the same place he had just got fired from, but I couldn't handle our cost of living on my own. We had to move out of the home with had made for ourselves. I saw how much it hurt him. I held all my emotions in, holding it together so we could figure out the next step. We moved in with his family this time and that's when people on the outside could see a little of what I had to deal with for years.

His family member asked if this type of behavior occurred often.

"Daily," I replied.

Without my knowledge, his family signed him up to go to a Christian rehabilitation center. When my husband and I found out about it, I was happy at first because he could finally get help and things would be better for us. But then I thought, *once again he gets to leave the mess he created, and I am left cleaning it up.* All the bitterness rose back up in my chest like heartburn. Forgiveness is a choice but the pain is an unwelcomed burden.

During this period, we were not getting along at all. I separated myself from Chip and went to stay with my mom. I was really at my breaking point with him. I needed and wanted a way out of this disaster called a marriage. My husband was against going into rehab and was upset with his family for signing him up. We met up to talk about it. After some convincing, he agreed that it was the best thing for him. On the day he left, I had so many conflicting emotions. I was happy, sad, angry, and confused about what was happening because it was going too fast to keep up with mentally.

The first two months he was away were hard to handle. I couldn't talk to him or see him. We would write letters almost every day. I couldn't imagine how he was feeling until I received the letters. I know I felt as if someone came and dropped a bomb in the middle of my life and left me cleaning up the aftermath. I knew that this was the best decision for him, but I felt a little selfish because I was still out here dealing with the world. I was still out here needing someone to swoop in and save the day. I was still very much alone and in need of some healing therapy too. I wanted to go somewhere and not have to worry about all the mess I left behind. Just focus on me, and when I returned, all would be swept up and put back in place, for me to rest my head in peace.

My heart calloused over.

Months went by and I will be honest, I was not a good wife. Yes, I made sure he had everything he needed and more. I saw him every chance I got, but mentally I had divorced him. My heart was no longer his. I had completely lost who I was with him. And now, without him.

Chapter 14

"Do You Know Me?"

Journal entry - *Spoken word*

"I am Not Who You Think"

I'm not who you think I am. I am a believer in Christ. I do believe that Jesus died so that I can have life. I believe that the Word was made flesh and dwelled among us (John 1:14). I believe that Jesus took the end of the life I had created for myself and made it the beginning of a life that is everlasting. Believing that He has done something for me that I could not have done for myself, knowing that He is my present help. Still, I am not who you think I am.

How the blessings continue to fall and most times I would not say thank you for them all. I never seem to forget you when I am in trouble, sowing seeds in my flesh not knowing that this can come back to me, double. I believe and trust the Holy Spirit and every word God has spoken over me. Still, I am not who you think I am.

If I say, "I believe, why do I question who I am?"

After treating Him with so much disrespect, reading His word, investing in my spirit, I seem to neglect.

I cannot wrap my mind around the fact that God could love me unconditionally. Not wanting to give up my old ways, I did what I thought was best. Quickly found out that you do not get more, going against God, you get less. Darkness created an illusion that seemed pleasing, forgetting that this feeling is only for a season.

The person that is now exposed, builds a foundation on her flesh. Now the flesh wants to react and blame others for my mess.

I called out to him to calm the storm, but it seemed He was not there. I was that one who wanted God to move when I thought He should. I was wrong. God moves on His timing because
we have no idea what we want or need. So, we must wait, this process determines how strong our faith is.

I hear a whisper "where is your faith? Remember you left me, and I have always been there. Am I who I say I am?"

When everything is said and done, I wonder where I am going. Is it Heaven or hell? Either way, at this moment I don't know. Darkness (flesh) versus Light (spirit), which one am I showing? All the seeds I have sown, whether good or bad, will harvest. No reason to be mad when I did it to myself. All I can do is ask God for help. So, I take a deep breath and keep going. I struggle daily to be more like you, Jesus. I say I want to be closer to you.
When you pull me in, it shows the real me and that's something I don't want people to see. Lord, I am so unworthy, this I know. I want my worship to be for real and not for a show.

I told you I am not who you thought I was. Why can't I walk in what I believe? If you see me fail or I allow my flesh to win, please do not judge me. Pray with me that God strengthens me to become the person I say I am...

(Read Romans 7)

(Mark 11:24, ESV)

"Therefore, I tell you, whatever you ask in prayer, believe that you have received it, and it will be yours."

(John 1:14, ESV)

"And the Word became flesh and dwelt among us, and we have seen his glory, glory as of the only son from the Father, full of grace and truth."

Food For Thought:

Do the people around you know the real you? Take some time to be real with yourself and talk to God about it. Confess to Him. He wants to hear from you. He knows you.

(1 John 1:9, ESV)

"If we confess our sins, he is faithful and just to forgive us our sins and to cleanse us from all unrighteousness."

Chapter 15

"Dead Woman Living"

I knew Chip was changing into a better man because his conversations were different. And that bothered me too. He was changing, but I was just the same. It was just too much damage on the inside to just hand over. While he was away, I should have been in preparation for what God was about to do. It was the right type of space I needed as well for me to get in tune and build a relationship with God so that he could give me the strength to endure. Instead, I ran rapidly in the opposite direction. Darkness had consumed me, and I felt that there was no turning back.

I wanted to get myself back right with God. I was ready. But being alone and trapped in my thoughts, took me further into a dark place. *How could I escape?* I wanted to say goodbye, but I was in too deep. Having sleepless nights, trying to pray, but it seemed as if God was not listening to me. I had returned to my old comforts, indulging in the company of people I knew were no good for me while I was in this state of mind. I was not okay and no one around me seemed to notice. That's when I felt like taking my own life. It would be easy. No one cared that I was a dead woman living. I just knew for sure no one would care if I was six feet under.

I tried it and didn't succeed. My cell rang and it was one of my friends calling. All I could do was cry. No words, just sobbing. I can truly say I was at my lowest point in life.

Journal entry - *Spoken word*

"Goodbye Darkness"

I'm between two worlds. One dimension. Trying to leave one and enter the other. Soon as I get one foot out and attempt to pull the other, I get snatched back into the old one. Could there be something in the old that I must take or leave? Maybe I am a tree that's planted where it's not supposed to be, in this battle between darkness and light.

Feeling as if there is no longer a reason to fight. So, I cried and searched the inner parts of my heart to find nothing but reasons to continue in the dark.

So I called it by name.

"Darkness, why cause so much pain to only realize nothing has changed? Darkness, you remember me when I was a scared weak minded little child? One who would do just about anything to make you proud? You made me feel like losing my little brother was all my fault."

"Brother, I said to myself repeatedly, that if I would have just left the permission slip on the table, you would have not gone on the field. You would still be here."

So deep in darkness, I danced for money as if I had been bought, lived reckless as if I had not been taught. Darkness blamed everything on the next person like Adam blamed Eve, lying to loved ones, trying to put their feelings at ease.

If I could tell the stories, darkness, how you blamed me when you touched me where only my husband was supposed to be. You have allowed me to feel so low at times with all the mixed emotions, had me thinking about taking death potions.

Playing with my mind. Pulling me away from men to women thinking that this was the best decision. Not knowing the whole time, darkness, keeping me close to you were your intentions. While you sit back and laugh at my failures, watching families tear each other apart because of what was done in the past.

Tearing relationships apart hoping they won't last.

I see your homeboy depression, Oh Yes! He played a major part, you guys worked hand and hand breaking my heart while pulling me farther away from what was safe. Confused about what to do, I didn't know my place.

Depression and darkness together had me thinking that life without me here would be better, it would give the people I had wronged time to forget that I existed. Those two together had me wanting to take my life. Thought about it. Not once but twice.

You know my History, not my Story. Being in darkness had me blinded to the power that lies deep within me. Not understanding who I am and how important my life is to everyone around me. And that my life is not just for me.

Felt weak and scared to show the real me. I knew I would be rejected, darkness promised that it would always protect me. Yeah, crazy as it sounds, I really believed, it could be.

I was sitting on the floor when that spoken word came to me. I kept reading it repeatedly. I knew I had to face the fact that I had been holding my husband captive, and myself as well. I knew I had to confess some things to him and just be open and honest. *How do I do this? Why should I confess something that I don't want to?* I hadn't considered all the damage it could do to others as well. I was scared and confused about what to do. I was only thinking about what was best for Asheley, not knowing it was not the best decision if the Holy Spirit wasn't in it. I have learned that a confession first must be made unto God, then allow him to lead you to the next step.

The time was drawing near for my husband to come home. After six months of being away, he was no longer the same man he was when he left. But I was some negatively altered version of the Asheley he had left behind. One thing's for sure, I was not who everyone thought I was.

63

Chapter 16

"The Prodigal Returns"

In a letter before Chip came home, I had confessed that I had lied and kept secrets in our marriage for so many years. *I didn't tell the lies to be rude or disrespectful*, I explained. It was just that I felt I was sparing feelings and didn't want to deal with the consequences that came behind it. The six-month period was over and now it was time to deal with the truth of all I had confessed to my husband face-to-face. Everything in me was like, *just leave and never look back.* But I didn't follow through with it. I stayed and toughed it out.

My husband arrived home with the knowledge of what I had done. I did not know what to think. Chip said nothing at first. But the next day, he started asking questions as if I were in an interrogation room waiting for evidence to prove I was guilty of much more. I kept avoiding the truth because I didn't know if the old Chip was still there or if he was completely gone. After hours of deliberation, He asked me to take him to the store. Chip returned to the car with beer. My heart sunk. I knew for sure things were about to explode.

On the way home from the store, Chip was quiet. He downed the first beer, and it seemed as if it opened another avenue in his mind. He was repetitive with the questioning. One turn after another, as if he could not get to the destination he was seeking. I stop responding. Either way, if I told a lie I was lying or if I spoke truthfully, I was lying. It had driven him so deep into a rabbit hole that he was asking *no return* questions. *Where did it happen? How many times? How has it?* Just things of a dark nature so he could torture himself. Keep reliving the hurt he was feeling.

I was exhausted. So, I stopped trying to spare his feelings. I just ripped the bandage right off. I gave him just what he was asking for. Every sickening detail he wanted. Of course, it made things worse. He resorted to calling family members and even our pastor to get advice about what to do. They would call me, and I was real with them. Like I said, I was fed up.

"Chip is feeling what I felt for years, and no one catered to how I felt! He goes to rehab and now everybody thinks he is a saint? Let's not forget all the times I went to sleep crying or not sleeping at all because I was scared to fall asleep thinking he might do something to me!"

I felt guilty for him drinking again, because of the situation I put us in. I knew I had to deal with the backlash of my decisions, and I was ready to take whatever I had coming to me. But I was not going to act like Chip's new lease on life just erased all of his messy past.

I was prepared to leave him or was fine with him leaving. But that was not the case. He looked me in the face one day and said, "I will not leave you because I love you. I committed to God, and I am keeping that promise. You are my wife and I am willing to work things out with you."

I knew God was in the midst of that because the old Chip couldn't have said anything like that!

At that moment, I felt God speak to me. *I have this same kind of love for you. If you would just trust that I have your marriage covered and you move out the way, you can be free.*

It reminded me of Luke 15:11-32, the story of the prodigal son. In the part where after the son returned home to his father, his father welcomed him with open arms. Had a party for him, and sat him at the table. Except I was the prodigal daughter. I could hear the Spirit of God say to me, *no matter what you have done against me I will still cover you underneath the covering, which is the blood of Jesus. I know you are a mess but if you will just come in anyway.*

That was amazing to me because no matter how far I kept straying away from God, He would always be there with open arms to take me back. That's the kind of love he has for us. That's the kind of love my husband had demonstrated to me. And it gave me confirmation that God was with him and in control of it all. He honestly left me speechless. My defenses slowly began melting away. Little did I know the whole time it was God saying, *look at me and not your problems.*

Chapter 17

"A Change Is Coming"

Journal entry - *God cares, meditation*

1 Peter 5:7 (ESV)

"Casting all your care upon him; for he cares for you."

My husband and I argued daily. He forgave me, but he no longer trusted me. I was okay with it because I felt that this was my fault and truthfully it was. I would talk to friends and family members about how to deal with all the damage that I caused, and no one seemed to have the answer I wanted. I was told to just wait on God and in due time, he would work it out. Others said, *hang in there it will get better.* The thing was, I didn't want it to get better. I was tired of this circus we called marriage and honestly, I just wanted it all to be over. I also felt as if God was not listening to me anymore, so I discarded all of that waiting on God stuff.

My wavering soul. As you can see, I was the epitome of a ship tossed back and forth. Some days I was, *God you have to take control.* Other days, I was back in my own way again. I tried to get ahead of the situation and fix it. I let my feelings and emotions get the best of me during the hard times in my life. Not only was I unfaithful to my husband, but most importantly to God, and I felt all the weight of that.

Journal entry - *Spoken word*

"Broken"

It felt like I was glass hitting the floor, pieces scattered everywhere. I know you see me lying here broken. Losing control of the slippery sculpture we call life. In the shadow hidden from the world, afraid of what it would do to me if they knew me. Seeing that no one noticed the smooth sides of the glass, only the sharp sides sting. Problems after problems wanted to escape but there was no way out.

I can still feel the warmth of the sun shining through the window. My mind, I no longer have control over. One thought to the next, this I cannot fix. The space felt empty. I know you see me lying here broken, and I know you hear me crying out.

Pick me up, you say. Tell me why I must try? I am broken, and no one has thought to ask me why. Then again, it doesn't matter in the end. Look at me, I'm all shattered.

Watching everyone in their blessing season, wondering why I am stuck in this season of lessons. Lord, am I not good enough? Lord, you say I am your child, how long do I have to wear this broken smile?

I hear a voice that tells me; my child you're blessed, I created you differently, you are not like the rest. All I need is for you to give me your best.

How can I be blessed when my life is a mess? Why am I the only one that must face all these tests?

My child you have been set apart, I had to break you to change your heart. Remember the miracle I performed with two fish and five loaves? How I blessed it, broke it, and gave it back to the people? And it multiplied, bringing sustenance to the earth. I waste nothing.

You are already blessed because you chose to live for me. Your vision was blurry, and you could not see. My reason for breaking you is to put you right where I needed you to be. In your brokenness, I can use you for my glory. And through you, others will see my faithfulness and power. I waste nothing.

The strength that is within you is greater than you will ever know. Only if you let my spirit have control. One of the things that block you is your pride. If I was to release you before your time you would have walked away from me.

Breaking you was needed, so understand that your trust should be in me only and not man. Pick up the pieces and place them in my hands. I will restore back to you the joy of your salvation and purify your heart. This is not the end but the beginning. Now, you can be who I have called you to be. Now, I can place you back into the world, while holding your head high and walking in the newness of life I have given to you.

I praised God for the revelation He had given me! Thanking Him in advance for the blessings to come, knowing that from this day forward, I would trust and depend on Him to see me through. The moments where we feel broken are the moments, we are the most powerful. We seek God with an open mind and humble heart because at this point our breakthrough is around the corner.

Chapter 18

"My Flesh on Life Support"

Two years passed by and you would have thought that it would have been a little better. It wasn't. Every time my phone made a noise, it was someone I was messing around with. Which was not true. Chip assumed the worse no matter how much I attempted to give my best. It had gotten to the point where I told my friends not to call or text after a certain time. I would have phone calls on speakerphone so he would know who I was talking to. I was so frustrated. I felt that I would have been better off if he would have just divorced me. This torment felt harder to deal with. One night after he had fallen asleep, I slipped outside. I sat in the car, smoking weed and crying out to God. It was not a prayer you would hear on a Sunday morning at church. It was a prayer that came from my soul.

All I remember saying was– *God, please help me get ME out of this! If you don't do something, I am going to lose my mind!* Afterward, all I could do was sob. I knew then that my flesh was on life support and she was fighting hard to live.

I walked back into the house and took a shower. While in there, I could hear God say, *first, you have to remove yourself out of the way.* He had said it to me before. But just like before, I didn't understand what he was saying to me. I got into bed and just laid there. Tears ran down my face and onto my pillow. My mind just racing. I was staring at the ceiling when Proverbs, three verse five kept coming to my mind. Now I didn't know what the scripture said so I got up and read it on my phone. I cried harder.

Journal entry - *Get out of my own way meditation*

PROVERBS 3:5 (ESV)
"Trust in the Lord with all your heart, and do not lean on your own understanding."

I just kept re-reading it and then I realized, this whole time I had been trying to fix something that I no longer had control over. Deep down, I loved my husband and I knew that he loved me. The circumstances made it so hard to see. I also knew that I should have been preparing myself for this storm. All I wanted to do was blame my husband for all this while he was away. I kept thinking, *if you were a real husband, to begin with, we would not have been in this situation in the first place.*

Then I also came to understand that if I loved God the way I said I did, I wouldn't have left myself open, falling into the lust of my eyes and flesh. God was who I should have been faithful to first. But no, I saw something different than what my husband was offering, and I wanted it. I didn't care if it was good or bad for me. I needed my flesh comforted because my soul was in misery. I talked myself into a lot of unforgiving things but couldn't seem to talk myself out.

I felt alone, so I started to write out all my feelings and frustrations about how guilty I felt. How I could not wrap my mind around the fact that my husband still wanted to stay with me. How I wanted everything to go away as if nothing happened. I was searching for a restart button and there was none. I wanted and needed a change badly. *But where to start? With everything and everyone but me.* Truth was, I was the problem. I started praying for a change.

One day as I was writing about how I needed a change, this is what the Spirit revealed to me.

Journal entry - *Spoken word*

"My God is Light"

Darkness, I can step into the light no matter how you try to convince me that I cannot. The light I now have will never leave nor forsake me. If I were you, I would disappear, because you are not welcomed here. Now I know with this light I no longer have the spirit of fear. He told me that I am more than a conqueror because I am in HIM. And my two feet "darkness and depression" are beneath them.

Now, watch me as I walk away with my head held high. Today is the day, I am saying goodbye. Living for and with Christ is my hunger. I now know with Jesus I am stronger. So in the next dimension, trust me when I say, you will not partake. Darkness, watch out because exposure is on the way and the power of it will give me sight.

Part III

~

Calming of the Storm

"A Renewed Mind"

Isolation is the perfect time for me to focus on you. I can clearly hear what you have for me to do. With all the commotion and calamity, it was hard for me to hear. But when I'm all by myself I can hear you whisper in my ear. Telling me, child, why run when I have something for you to do. I hear you Lord, so I'm trusting you.

You know you were called and purposed so you need to go to work. But Lord, what would everybody say? They know my dirt. Just do what I told you to do and everything is going to work out. Oh yea, of little faith. Why do you doubt?

Okay, Father. I hear you and I do understand. I was created for this. I am part of your master plan. Thank you, Lord, for talking with me. Thanks for all the time. I'm ready to go now, Father. I have a renewed mind.

A Poem By: Lee O. Barnes Jr. (Chip)

Chapter 19

"A Reflection: What is Change?"

Journal entry - *Notes on Change*

Can someone tell me when you change the situation you are in? Will it start when you are tired of going through the same things over and over? Or when everything you have worked hard for just falls apart right before your eyes? Do you change then?

Honestly, I cannot answer that for anyone.

The mind is the first place that comes under attack. That is where everything begins. Our thought process is where a lot of our mistakes in life come from. We sit and ponder on a thought until we speak on it. Next, we are acting on it. Before we realize it, the thought becomes reality whether it was good or bad. Either way, it starts in your mind. That is why the scripture says that we must not think like the world but change our mindset to Christ and do the will of the Father.

The change in my life started once I confessed all my hidden issues and tried to figure everything out on my own. I gave my life to Christ again for the third time. With little to no understanding of what salvation meant. I was thinking that every time I sinned that I needed to be saved again. Now I have learned that once you are saved by grace it is that same grace that keeps you saved. I want to be able to be taught by a leader who loves God. Salvation was the best thing, but learning and understanding what it means was life-changing.

After writing this, I was still feeling broken. Some days I said, *God please give me strength.* The next day, I thought, *I cannot do this.* My two natures intertwined and struggled to break free. With everything going on with my husband and me, there was no way things were going to get better. At least this is what I told myself. I said it so much, that I began to believe it. It was manifesting right before my eyes.

I was wanting a change right now and it felt like God was taking too long. We were still fighting. I was still being accused of things I was no longer doing. He was still drinking again. My attitude was worse than before. I asked God, *why isn't this working?* He just softly spoke to me; *you are still in the way.* I could not see or just did not want to see that it was me because I kept putting blame on others and trying to make excuses for my actions. There was none!

I was afraid too because now everyone knew that I had cheated on my husband. And to make matters worse, it was someone he knew. I was trying to get my husband to leave me. Just get it over with and end both our misery. I started telling him about old affairs that happened back when we were in the other city. I told him that I never loved him.

"I'm not in love with you now!" I shouted. Just constantly putting fuel to the fire.

This man took all that (*no one but God, because I knew how the old Chip would have reacted*). He looked at me for a moment with disbelief in his eyes. I felt he hurt. Part of me wanted to just die. The other was laughing because now he could feel what I had been feeling all through the years. I did not intentionally do it out of spite, I told myself. I saw it as the seeds he sowed over the years.

He looked at me. With ache, fury, and determination in his eyes, passionate and pained words erupted, "*I am not going anywhere! Because I promised God that I would love you and he told me to stay. That is what I'm doing.*"

I rolled my eyes and walked out of the room. *I give up, nothing is working*, I thought. I just wanted to be alone again in my misery. It was the first time I felt stress-free, at least that's what I told myself *that* was. I was back to the drawing board, trying to come up with an escape plan. And again, I hear God say, *YOU ARE IN THE WAY!!*

Those words nagged at me, frustrating my mind more. *How was I in the way*? I still could not see it. I kept thinking about how to change this but that's not what God wanted. But it was still what I wanted.

Chapter 20

"A Reflection: How to Change"

Journal entry - *What to do when it's time for a change?*

Can you change your name, color your hair, or even move to another state just to hide who you are inside? Sad to say, it will not change anything. What if people knew the "real" you? I am talking about the person that you battle with daily. That person who sneaks around, lies, is filled with anger, holds on to past hurt, and blames self for every failure in your life. The person you keep everyone else from seeing.

What if people knew that person? Would your life be better or worse? I sit and think about how many people would walk away from me if they knew the real me. In my flesh, I have a lot of anger, anxiety, and so many other mixed emotions that I kept hidden from the world. I tend to lie about things just to spare the feelings of others. It's easy for me to quit and give up, doubt myself, and fear has taken control over me. During this storm, dealing with confessing my wrongs to my husband, I forgot that I never confessed them to God.

I have also battled with temptations. I could have kept my feelings to myself about this other guy and asked God to help me. Instead, I reacted to what my flesh wanted and failed. Many things I have done in my flesh that were shameful to tell anyone, holding on to guilt and not sure how to let it go. What is stupendous about our God is that none of these matter. He will always be there to walk with me through it all. No matter how big or small the storms of life may seem. Our God is bigger than them all. Still, in this moment of my life, I couldn't recognize that.

It was my Spirit talking to me while I was writing. It blew my mind to know that God would still commune with me after all I had done against my husband (my mind was still in the wrong place). I kept focusing on me wronging him and him wronging me. I never really took the time to acknowledge that it was *God* the entire time I was lying to, cheating on, and disrespected. My husband and I played the blame game for another year. Yep, another full year of distrust, and fighting, to realize that somebody must grow up spiritually. I was not Ms. Perfect, and he was not Mr. Right, and we knew that. But our minds were not in the right place to see that we both were the problem.

The problem was, that the beginning of our marriage was built on a foundation of what we thought and felt instead of what God required of us. One Sunday during couples' class, I heard something that opened my eyes. There was an older couple there and the husband commented: *"If we would evaluate ourselves and stop trying to fix our spouses how we want them to be and just let God work on us individually, we would have many successful marriages."*

A light bulb came on in my head. The teacher's study focused on how Adam and Eve did the blame game back in the Bible days. Adam blamed Eve, Eve blamed the snake. All God wanted was for Adam to take responsibility for it because he oversaw everything. When we got home, I kept meditating on what I had heard at church. Chip was doing something outside, so I used this chance to talk to God. I repented for the things I knew I had done and for whatever sins I didn't know I had committed. I suddenly felt a weight lifting off me. I opened the Bible app on my phone and just started reading. It was not a certain book or chapter. Whatever came up first is what I read. As I was reading,

Chip walked back inside. He made some snide comment about how I hadn't been reading, *why now?*

I ignored the sarcastic and petty remarks he gave to focus on the glimmer of light that was growing in me. I kept my composure and continued to read. That day, I let go and let God have everything because I was tired of playing God, trying to fix this on my own.

I was asking God to speak to me and show me what I needed to do to endure all this hardship that I caused. This scripture came to me.

Journal entry - *Wait on God meditation*

(Psalm 30:5b, KJV)
Weeping may endure for a night, but joy comes in the morning.

Chapter 21

"Morning's Coming"

I knew that I had shed enough tears and it was time to get my joy back. Sometimes your morning may not be the next day. It may be weeks or even years before God opens a way for you. During that time, we still need to seek him daily. That is what I started to do, seek God for myself and build a real relationship with him. Once I had done those things, it was a little better. God didn't change the situation I was in, but he taught me through the Spirit to view my situation differently. I stopped looking and thinking about all the things I had been through or had done to my husband. Instead, I focused on what was required of me from God. Equipped with this new outlook, I was able to move along just fine.

Journal entry - *The power of light meditation*

THE POWER OF LIGHT - JESUS

(Psalm 21:1, ESV)

"The Lord is my light and my salvation; whom shall I fear? The Lord is the stronghold of my life; of whom shall I be afraid."

After stepping into the light everything was exposed, even the secrets that I never would have told. Once again, afraid of losing people that were close to me, at that moment with my spiritual eyes I could not see. God spoke to me through the Holy Spirit, saying where I am taking you no one else can go. The people and things you are holding on to, LET IT GO.

After hearing these words, it did not register to me what the Lord was saying. When I finally grasped what it was, it was hard for me to let it go. I had become so accustomed to that lifestyle that everything else seemed out of place. Giving up my old life hurt, but I'd gain so much more in return, to live for Jesus.

I had to put Asheley in the dirt. That was to give up any and everything pleasing to me and not God. Now, I understand that Jesus is the only way, the truth, and the light. No one can see God without seeing Jesus first. Grateful for His blood that covers us day and night.

(John 14:6, ESV) Jesus said to him, "I am the way, and the truth, and the life. No one comes to the Father except through me."

I used to be shackled by darkness, not bold enough to admit it when things began to get rough. The first thing I wanted to do was quit. When my eyes began to open spiritually, I knew then I had to submit. Submit to the will of God and not my own. The light I found healed the sick and gave sight to the blind, not forgetting the water He turned into wine. This light, if you let Him, will renew and ease a troubled mind. He will take you just the way you are, no matter if you're near or far.

This Light is my advocate to the Father in Heaven. Without Him in my life, I would not be able to approach God myself. With the power the light has given me, I can tear down strongholds and break generational curses. I can love you even if I do not receive it back. If you have hurt me, with this Light I can uplift you. Even someone that purposely tore me down.

Now, on my face, I wear a smile instead of a frown. See, this Light gives me strength in my weakness. Gives me an understanding of temperance and meekness. I have been blessed more than I deserve. Now I choose to be a witness.

To tell the good news of Jesus (death, burial, resurrection) of what I have been taught. My path now is bright, no longer going left when God tells me to go right. With my hands lifted, all I can say is thank you Jesus for being this light and more.

(John 8:12, ESV) "Again Jesus spoke to them saying, "I am the light of the world. Whoever follows me will not walk in darkness but will have the light of life."

Life still gave me trials. Some I passed, and some I failed, understanding that grace and having faith that God can do the impossible was enough motivation for me. My husband was away for a while during this point of my life, and everything I thought I knew was put to the test He wrote a poem called "On This Journey".

After reading it, I realized that we all are unworthy of God's grace, but He gives it to us anyway. Brand new each day. I am so grateful that through all the bad situations, I put myself in before and after salvation, He was still there willing to forgive me and give me another chance to get it right. Thank you, Jesus!!

God will isolate you from your surroundings, so He can talk with you. We do not like it when God takes everything we hold so close to us away. But that is the only way He can get some of our attention. During this isolation period, God can use and speak to us or simply use it to just get our focus back to Him. As we go through our daily tasks, we should take time out to give God glory. Not for what He has blessed us with, but simply because He is God alone. Because He deserves it, and much more....

Food for Thought:

Think about a time God had to isolate you for a while for Him to commune with you. How was that experience for you?

Chapter 22

"Better Days Ahead"

I had to go back and tear down the foundation I had built on my own to rebuild with God as he instructed me to. Was it easy? No, it was truly a struggle. I was only on the first step–surrendering all. I didn't know what *all* meant, but I kept trusting God and believing that better days were coming.

When you're at that point where you have talked with everyone you can think of for advice. And it seems nothing is helping. You realize all the while, that it was God whom you needed to go to all along. Once He has your focus back to Him, now he can use you how he wants. But we must endure and wait on God for instructions on what to do next. It will not be easy, but if we suffer with Christ, we will reign with Him. I told myself, *I am encouraging you to hold on and don't give up. In the meantime, give God all the Glory for this storm. After all, it was to grow you spiritually and to draw you closer to God.*

This storm was a test of my endurance and if I was the person, I said I was. It made me evaluate my life and my relationship with Christ and on a grading scale I was an "F"! I had to start denying the things I wanted to react to, and humble myself so God could have control. Once I surrendered, it still seemed as if things were not getting better.

The lightning seemed to persist. The roar of thunder we both felt on the inside while trying to reconcile with each. The point of not knowing if we would stay together or divorce. But knowing we had to hold on. The downpour of the rain, when living day to day with guilt, and shame. The more we wanted to just put it behind us, still the more we were being constantly reminded. Arguments and disrespect from us both. I had little to no faith or fight in me to want to continue. But I had to. I did not know how God was going to fix this. It looked so bad from my view. I sometimes felt that it was even too big for God. Deep down, I knew it was bigger than me, but I was not sure how to fully move out of the way. I kept attending church, Bible class, and reading on my own. I was determined to strengthen my relationship with Christ. I saw some changes and clung to every glimmer of light I could. I badly wanted God to change my situation and just erase this part of my life. Wake me up when it was over. But he only helped me to see myself for who I am. *It had to start with me!*

My flesh was putting up a fight. I still had moments where I would react instead of moving proactively. But my spirit-man would remind me that I am no longer that person. I am a representation of Christ. I had my old way of thinking butting heads with the new person I was becoming. Battling with the two, I grew frustrated. I was still focused on what I was dealing with but God kept showing me who I was and the things I needed to deny to follow him. God had me right where he wanted me, or rather, right where I needed to be. I had to listen. I dug in, facing *Me vs Me….*

Chapter 23

"Say Bye to Your Flesh"

Journal entry - *Flesh vs Spirit meditation*

Romans 8:5(ESV)

"For those who live according to the flesh set their minds on the things of the flesh, but those who live according to the Spirit set their minds on things of the Spirit."

Praying for God to show me the next door, not knowing it was something I was not ready for. Wanting to obey his every word battling between many voices in my head. Trusting God for directions made me realize that my flesh can't stay any longer. Now putting her to death is not easy, there was no way I could do it alone. With Jesus, I knew I would remain strong. He will and always has given me the strength to go on. Now it's time to stop running from Him and run to Him.

If you think that denying yourself will be easy it will not. Because, in this body, we battle with sinful lusts. Sometimes, we do not realize that we are doing them. Then other times, we do them because we like how it makes our flesh feels.

1 John 2:16:17(KJV)
"For all is in this world, the lust of the flesh and the lust of the eyes and the pride of life, is not from the Father, but is of the world. And the world passes away."

Journal entry - *Spoken word*

"No Longer Belong to Self"

It is time to rise and be who God is calling me to be. No more playing around. The law no longer has a hold on me.

My eyes and ears are finally open. Unworthy of His grace but still, I'm chosen. No one could take His place. If I had to do what he did for me, I wouldn't have shown my face.

Surrender all to Christ. After all, he is the ultimate sacrifice, so that you and I could have life more abundantly and have life for eternity. With my head up and a smile on my face, knowing that I am saved through grace by faith.

It is time to trust God's plan. Stop asking for his hand and receive his heart. It's time to renew your mind and leave the past behind. Having knowledge, wisdom, and understanding; following Jesus and doing what he is commanding.

It is time to have faith like Abraham, believing God will provide in the bush, there is my ram. Serving the same God that controls the seas, the same God that washed me clean and set me free.

Time to understand the true meaning of the cross, Lord, give me strength to help the ones who are lost. Eyes to see and ears to hear. Lord, it's time for me to do your will. So when I want to run, allow me to be still and trust you. With all power in your hands, when I feel like giving up, please help me to just stand. Stand on your promises and the blessings you have given. Sometimes my flesh is weak, but my spirit is always willing.

Jesus, you are the way, the truth, and the light. When my flesh arises, your word is what I use to fight. I now know that it is not a fight in the flesh but a battle in the spirit. So, I am calling on your name, praying that you hear me. We walk by faith and not by sight so when I face trials that are going to come, I might not see the outcome or see the way. But God, your will is what I am trusting day by day. The blood you shed, nothing can top that. All I want is to get my relationship with you back. Thank you, Jesus, for catching all the slack. Because with you, there is no turning back.

Chapter 24

"God, Work on Me!"

Calming of the storm is the process where you just sit back and let God work on you and your situation. That is when I began to operate in faith and not fear.

In everything we go through, we must praise God continually and thank Him for His grace and mercy that he gives to us daily. As believers of Christ, we must remember that our problems nor the storms of life are not bigger than our God! We can hold our heads up and keep moving forward, for greater is coming.

Journal entry - *Faith meditation*

(Hebrews 11:1, KJV).
"Now faith is the substance of things hoped for, evidence of things not seen."

When we start seeing God move in our lives our first thought is materialistic things. We fail to recognize the small things He has blessed us with, that we take for granted, that has the most value. How many of us wake up in the morning and thank God for the trees outside, the grass, and even the birds of the sky? Or thank Him for just simply giving you air in your lungs to breathe? It is things like this that we do not take time out to notice and be thankful for. After all, God created it all.

(Read - Genesis 1:1)

As believers of Christ, we must understand that we are unworthy of God's grace, which should break our hearts. Yet still, in our imperfections, we serve a perfect God. We come to understand that God loves us so much that he gave His only begotten son (*John 3:16)* so that you and I could have a second chance to get it right! Wow! What an amazing God we serve! So just take this moment and ask yourself, *if God has done all of this for us, what have we done for Him lately?*

Often, we say that we trust God until we are tested or put ourselves in a situation that gives us no choice but to trust Him. Even then, we try to find the easy way out. The first thing we forget about is the word He has spoken over our lives. And how to use the faith we say we have.

This is what I did. I talked as if I had faith bigger than the next person until a trial came. My reaction to the trials revealed that I was all talk and no walk. I did not want to trust the process that God had already worked out the situation for me, instead of trusting His timing I wanted things to change right away.

I complained and did things out of my will thinking I could move faster than God, feeling as if I had all the answers to my problems. I was just telling God that I did not need Him. Later, I found out that all I needed was *Him*. This lead me right back to the beginning, asking for His help to get me out of something I got myself into. (*I know I am not the only one who has been there before*).

Faith is believing that you already have something before you obtain it. We use faith every day in our daily lives for tangible things, but when it comes to using our faith spiritually, we tend to forget how it works. We act that way with Jesus as well. When everything is going just right, we do not study, or commune with God. We won't even attend church services and Bible class. Soon as a trial arrives, here we go praying: *"Lord I have faith that you will get me out of this…"*

All this while forgetting that you had not given your spirit anything to work with. God's word tells us that faith without work is dead. There are many faith examples in the

Bible. My favorite is Abraham. He is an example of faith using works.

(Read Genesis 22)

Abraham did not have everything in his life together, but he was obedient to God and believed in Him.

(James 2:17, ESV)
"So also, faith by itself, if it does not have works, is dead."

When Christ becomes our central focus, our faith in Him becomes stronger. It is not an overnight process. It takes time and dedication, with meditation on the Word. Right now, we may not know where we are going or how we are going to make it. But faith in Jesus and the words He has spoken over us will give us that push we need to keep going. The situation you are in right now may seem as if it's not going to change but it will. All we must do is tell God and trust that He has worked everything out for our good.

(Romans 8:28, ESV)
And we know that for those who love GOD all things work together for good, for those who are called according to His purpose.

Chapter 25

"A Renewed Mind"

Journal entry - *Renew your mind meditation*

Romans 12:2 (KJV)

"And be not conformed to this world; but be ye transformed by the renewing of your mind, that ye may prove what is that good and acceptable, and perfect, will of God."

The renewing of your mind (changing the way we think, and view situations) is a process. It will not happen overnight. We have been using the old mindset for as long as we can remember. So when you try to do things differently, the old way will fight against it. That is why we must invest in the new mind (in the Spirit) by reading the word of God, going to Bible class, etcetera. Understand that life's problems will not go away but the Holy Spirit will help you along the way.

I remember the time when I stopped investing and allowed what I was going through to be bigger than God, thinking I could fix and handle life's tests on my own. No, it did not work. What I'd done was made things worse, things began to spin out of my control. At that point, I had no other choice but to turn back to Him.

Before I fully grasped that it is life-changing to invest, the fire I had, to run for God, slowly began to die down. This happened because I started thinking back in my old mindset and doing my own thing again. Not knowing that I would be tested. Every test that came, I failed. I had no *Word* in me. Therefore, the Holy Spirit had nothing to work with. So, what I had in me came out. None of it was spiritual because I was feeding the old way of thinking (flesh) rather than feeding the new way of thinking (spirit).

See, it was like being in high school. The teacher tells you the information that's being provided for you is important, so pay attention. And you will be tested on it. The same thing applies when it comes to life. God has given us everything we need to pass the test. It is up to us to gather the information. I wondered why all these things were happening and why it was so hard to maintain through it all. So many times, I wanted to give up because my flesh was stronger than my spirit-man. In other words, I was always in my feelings and on the defensive about everything. All the while, I was going to church and Bible class. Doing things outwardly for others to think I had it together. I had to step back and do a reality check on myself and face the fact that I was not the person I was pretending to be.

One day, I was laying on the couch and thinking about how I had been lying to myself and others. Most importantly, lying to God. On the outside, I looked like a believer in Christ, but when life's trials began to occur they showed me something different about myself.

Journal entry - *Spoken word*

"Open Heart"

It is easy to say, Lord, I surrender, with a heart that is not tender. When it's time to walk, I freeze. With no words, I can't talk. Could it be that I am scared or maybe hard of heart? Either way, giving up the old me, was I ready to truly part? Trying to stay focused and my mind steady, times I wanted to give up, but the Spirit would not let me go. There is a fight in me and praise that needs to come out. Not talking about a scream or a shout. In my life, being obedient to God's word, true worship comes from a pure heart of truth. With an open heart and a changed mind, I now know what I must do. My heart desires to be more like you.

Set my soul on fire! Show your glory to me! In you, I know I can be free! Your life, you gave for me. With an open heart, I am redeemed from what was possessing me.

My testimony. I will share how you loved me. Through it all, you had always been there. Tearing down walls, I had built on a slippery slope of guilt. Trying to wrap my mind around how can you still use me! After knowing what I have done, guess that's the love you are trying to get me to embrace. Show me how to share your grace. My heart is open, wherever you lead me, Lord, I am willing to walk!

Chapter 26

"He Calms the Storm"

During the calming period of my storm, it was strange. Something completely out of the ordinary. Everything was in shatters, and I did not have anywhere to go but to God. That's when my eyes came open to see that the whole time I was not alone. With all the teaching and reading on my own, I still found myself feeling down and discouraged. Or even scared, not knowing what to do or where to go. In Matthew 8:24-26, the disciples were afraid during the storm they were in, and the whole time, Jesus was asleep.

They thought among themselves how can this man sleep, and we are in the midst of the biggest storm in a boat! With little to no understanding of what to do, the disciples called out to Jesus for help. That sounds so familiar. As believers today, we still do the same. And what I love about the Matthew passage is that when the disciples awake Jesus and tell him about the storm, he calmly replies, *"where is your faith?"*

Faith in Jesus. That He has already calmed the storm for me! Jesus spoke a word to the wind and sea, and it calmed. All I needed to do, was speak *The Word* over my situation and have faith that God's words would calm our storm!

I've seen myself in the position of Jesus's disciples, at times during my storm. I found myself personalizing it instead of using faith to get me through it. Not realizing that all God was doing was teaching me to use my faith instead of fear. So, I would panic and call out for Him to stop the storm. Little did I know, that I would face it again.

I encourage you to stop elevating your problems and elevate God. He is the only one who can and will navigate you through any life storm that may occur. Just like the disciples had to go through another storm, the difference is that this time they used their faith. The only one who was bold enough to walk out on faith was Peter. Peter walked on water to get to Jesus, but he was distracted and began to sink, and once again they were afraid.

In today's time as believers, we sink because we take our eyes off Jesus. We tend to listen to our best friends, or someone we think is spiritual instead of waiting on the voice of God. Let's stay focused on Christ, the author, and finisher of our faith. Trusting that this storm and all others to come, we will get through them as long as our foundation is based on Christ.

While in our flesh, we are bold, doing whatever it is we love doing against God. I can recall while I was in my storm, I did not know how long I would be in it nor did I know what to expect after it was over. And that is what scared me the most. So, if you are feeling fearful about the next step, let me share with you how Christ gave me the strength to endure the storm.

I got out of the way!

Fighting through my fears, I trusted Him. And he worked everything out according to His will and purpose.

Chapter 27

"I Am a New Creation"

Journal entry - *Becoming a new creature in Christ meditation*

(2 Corinthians 5:17, KJV)
"Therefore, if any man be in Christ, he is a new creature; old things pass away; behold, all things are become new."

In the middle of me trying to figure everything out on my own, making a mess of my life in the process, I was operating in my old nature. I did not walk fully into the person God was molding me to become. Becoming a new creature in Christ took a lot of studying and meditation on the word of God.

(Galatians 2:20, ESV)
I have been crucified with Christ. It is no longer I who live in the flesh I live by faith in the son of God, who loved and gave himself for me.

When we say that we are born again in Christ Jesus, there are things that we can no longer partake in because it is out of the will of God. We are used to our old way of thinking and living. So much so, that when a trial comes, we revert to our old ways because that is a familiar place for us.

There was a period in my life after I accepted Christ to be my personal savior, I still felt like I could continue in my old way of thinking. I felt like I knew enough about Jesus that I could still do what I wanted and not face the consequences of my actions against God. I needed to learn his Word and precepts. I was frustrating the grace of God. I drew baseless conclusions, determining that I would be forgiven because I had accepted Christ into my life. Therefore, I could still do those things I had done before.

(Romans 6:1-4, KJV)
"What shall we say then? Shall we continue in sin, that grace may abound?
God forbid. How shall we, that are dead to sin, live any longer therein?
Know ye not, that so many of us as were baptized into Jesus Christ were baptized into his death?
Therefore, we are buried with him by baptism into death: that like as Christ was raised from the dead by the glory of

the Father. Even so, we also should walk in the newness of life."

I began to see myself one day, in third person. I could see my flesh side, at this point was the strongest) and I could see my spirit-man, slowly fading out of sight! As I watched the two, I could clearly see where I was in both worlds. I was seeing the two natures in a battle right before my eyes! I became determined to strengthen my spirit that day and die to the old self. To this day, it is still quite a journey. But my vision is clearer, and my mind is stronger.

There are so many things I can relate to during my walk with Christ that most of you are dealing with. I can tell you that it is harder to deal with if we do not understand who Jesus is and who we are in Him. Most of us struggle in different areas of our life and are not sure how to handle them. We want to confide in people but are not sure who we can trust with that type of information.

Well, I have good news. God already sees and understands everything we have gone through! Going to the right people (that has a relationship with God) can help when you need counsel. But, once we grasp that we can go to God for ourselves because Jesus has given us the ability to approach God without Judgement, we will no longer depend solely on our support group.

I still have days when I must push harder than others. We all fall short from time to time, but God's grace and mercy are what's keeping us. His love is a kind that will never fail. Although we are saved, we still are in the flesh. So, we must make up in our minds that we are going to deny ourselves and live for God and Him alone. The cares of this world will overtake us if we are not spiritually strong to endure. That's where our *Faith* comes in. Yes, we will still fight against the lust of the eye, the pride of life, and any other enticing thing our flesh may desire. But, when we invest in our spirit and sow to the spirit, then we will have allowed God to take control.

Chip and I are still together and our love for each other is stronger than ever! We had to realize that only God can fix the brokenness we had in our marriage. Things started turning around once we stopped looking at each other's faults, stopped blaming one another, and took responsibility for our actions. I can truly say that when we begin to love each other as Christ loves us, it made it easier to be submissive.

I pray that my testimony and the trials I faced will help you to see that you are not alone. As the body of Christ, we are here to help and encourage one another to keep the faith and stand up for what and who we believe in.

As I continue to grow in the Spirit, I ask that you all will continue to pray with me that God will strengthen me to stand on His word and live for Him.

Thank you, for taking the time to read this book. I pray that it will be a blessing to you in many ways! God gets all the glory because these are the words, He placed in me to give unto you. Peace be with you. May God continue to strengthen each of you as you build a relationship with Him.

Be blessed beloved! Until we meet again, my God bless you according to His will!

Love your sister in Christ,

Asheley Barnes

Acknowledgments

LORD, thank you for blessing me with a gift of writing, and a chance to use this gift to glorify you. I ask that you touch every person that reads this book. Lord, I pray that their eyes and ears will come open to hear and see you for who you are. Father, I give thanks and acknowledge your Holy Spirit, because none of this would be possible without him. Grant us an understanding of your will for our lives and we will be careful to give you all the praise and honor that is due to your Holy name. Thank you, Lord, for everything.

In Jesus' name, Amen.

Primeira parte

Na pele de outra

1.

Prémices

Por uma bonita noite de inverno, neste do princípio de janeiro, após cerca de horas merecidas bem sono profundo, terríveis dores apreendem-se violentamente do meu pulso direito. Numerosas quitações elétricas encarceram-me e impedem-me dormir. Massagens do meu antebraço não podem nada em frente de este violento ataque brusco e repetido do invasor. Uma dor sem ninguém outro similar, que lança de repente, queima intensamente à lugar onde age no meu corpo que não pode opôr-se aos eletrochoques. É impossível pensar de esperar que as dores passam em cerca de dias. O embaraço é assim potente e original que prometo-me que torne-se no meu não especialista na manhã.

Qual consagrado presente o ano dos meus quarenta anos! Sinto-me no entanto jovem e ainda cheio de energia.

Qual disfuncionamento corporal significa este mal? Da parte superior do meu metro sessenta e três, tem uma morfologia fina com os meus cinquenta e quatro quilogramas. É louro com cabelos longos terminados. Não tenho nada de um desportista, se não for o andamento.

O meu não especialista pede-me que faça um exame, électromyogramme ligado ao canal carpien, à investigação do seu disfuncionamento. Testemunha da compressão do nervo a nível do pulso.

O resultado é negativo. Bem ter-me-ia passado deste exame doloroso composto de agulhas e de quitações elétricas tanto quanto o especialista indicou-me que a minha polegada não atingida por perturbações de sensibilidade, o exame era inúteis.

Cerca de dias atrasado, e a análise biológica em mão, o diagnóstico cai sobre "que tranquiliza" inflamação muscular sem origem específica, sem motivo médico aparente e sem solutionnement. Os CPK e aldolase são anormalmente elevados.

Enquanto que a inflamação muscular encarcera rapidamente a integralidade do meu corpo, imobilizando os meus membros inferiores e superiores, é o início do meu constrangimento físico! Um horror a viver, suportar e gerir!

Passo por várias fases em cerca de dias: o medo atenaza-me. Seguidamente interrogações invadem o meu cérebro. Que chega-me? Porque mim? O que fez para merecer aquilo? Qual é a gravidade? É o início do fim? Como viver com? Como evolui a doença? Como gerir-o? Que vai tornar-se a minha se for caso disso rapariga? ... Qual galère!

 Contra todo, sou uma que bate e mim não aceito o meu triste destino. Não quero ser doente. Penso à uma inflamação provisória e não dou qualquer minha confiança ao corpo médico que hesita, testa e procura.

É suficiente imaginar-me, jovem mulher de quarenta anos com fortes dores físicas misturadas uma uma mobilidade corporal extremamente reduzida.

O meu não especialista não tem diagnóstico preciso nem de solução médica a propôr-me se não for uma hospitalização de uma semana para exames médicos. Nenhum tratamento foi-me dado. Único o tempo dará os sinais concretos médicos para remediar: um dia, uma semana, um mês, três meses... Ninguém não sabe! Permaneço na incerteza mais total. Uma biópsia muscular deveria ser programada mas não quero exame intrusif sem dúvida puxada por uma mistura de medo e de dor. A opção fechada ao hospital durante uma semana para exames não me parece acessível. Sou então uma jovem mamã de uma criança de dezasseis meses. Não o retenho. É o início de investigações infinitas que vão durar de numerosos anos ao meu grande desespero.

As minhas dores acentuam-se ao fio das semanas e o meu não especialista, consciente deste estado de facto, não pode nada trazer-me. Giro-me para o reumatologista, que diagnostica um fibromyalgie e prescreve um tratamento antibiótico, seguidamente tendo em conta a ineficácia, um tratamento anti-inflamatório, seguidamente o paracetamol com codeína: sem resultado convincente.

Não posso acreditar que o fibromyalgie é uma doença da qual a origem é desconhecido, que não pode ser parada nem aliviada e cuja impotência do corpo médico é posta à dia.

Os meses vão-se embora no calendário e as dores opõem-se sempre e fazem do meu corpo um zombie porque não responde mais às minhas solicitações desde demasiado muito tempo. Com efeito, a minha esperança de uma inflamação provisória começa a diminuir-se. Deve fazer-me à ideia de ser doente à vida? Em cerca de meses, a minha resistência diminui-se. O meu dinamismo solta-se que deixa o lugar à uma lentidão e sobretudo profundas limitações do conjunto dos meus movimentos.

O cansaço teve razão da minha vida social, familiar e profissional. À extremidade de um ano de cansaço, esgotava-me fisicamente. A minha mãe alertava-me no entanto frequentemente sobre a minha perda de pesos mas recusava entender-o. Pacientava dos dias melhores. Via-me diferente do olhar do outro. No entanto, era assustada pela minha perda de pesos espetacular. Em quatro meses, tinha a impressão de jogar ao jackpot dos quilos. E um, dois, três, e quatro quilos menos! Cinco, seis, sete, oito!!! Então perdi dez quilos! O meu irmão mais velho, arreliador às suas horas, comparou-me mesmo, na sua grande bondade, "à Auschwitz". À sua partida, chorei todas as lágrimas do meu corpo. Tinha com efeito apenas a pele sobre os meus ossos. Os ossos da minha bacia furavam à vista de olho a minha pele, o colar de ossos em redor do meu pescoço acentuava-se, o meu rosto décharnait, as minhas faces escavavam-se, os meus braços assemelhavam-se a um boneco articulado... O todo acentuado por um ferro fundido muscular espetacular. Os meus quarenta e quatro quilos levavam-me para um declínio físico irreversível se não me tomasse em carga rapidamente. Apesar da minha obstinação a ver nada, tinha o sentimento de ter uma silhueta de manequim! Queria ao mesmo tempo proteger a minha família das minhas perturbações físicas e évertuais esconder-lhes a triste realidade, muito confortando-se na esperança quase imatura de dias melhores onde a minha saúde retomaria a parte.

Por conseguinte tornei-me no meu novo não especialista em janeiro para alertar-o da minha descida aos infernos seguidamente em abril para pedir-lhe que ajude-se porque não podia mais haver único. Como é difícil pedir ajuda! Mas a urgência era como não podia fazer diferentemente. Sentia-me impotente. Não tinha mais a força de reagir. Não conhecia a saída de socorros. Não me sentia corajoso. Perdia as minhas forças. Não chegava a guiar a minha vida de adulto convenientemente como sempre fiz-o. Era mãe e responsável da minha progenitura. Devia aumentar-se e fazer face. Mas como? Nenhum médico compreendia a minha desordem. Nenhuma solução concreta foi-me trazida. A minha mãe dava-me bem às vezes restos de pratos cozinhados. Transformado em objeto de curiosidade, fora de normas, o meu estado de saúde era incompreensível para comum do mortais. E no entanto, bem real para mim que vivia-o à cada respiração!

O que teria sido necessário estes em momentos de solidão? A dor física é imensa, mesmo abissal! A isolamento, a solidão, o sentimento de ser único no seu canto, a sensação de não ter nenhuma porta de saída, de ter errado a minha vida, encontrar-me basicamente do buraco, não avançar, roçar o imobilismo, não aproveitar da vida, a não ser compreendido, não servir à nada, ser velho e feio, ser inútil e enfezado, ser um abismo e um desperdício para a sociedade! Os tanto pensamentos negativos invadiam a minha cabeça. O meu espírito parecia mais apenas obstruído por esta consagrado doença. Cada gesto trazia-me à ela. Cada segundo vivia através de ela.

É fácil este em sentido abandonar-se à doença e o corpo médico, enfiar-se nos sapatos do paciente e deixar-se guiar. Aceitar-se como tal não é a boa diligência ao meu sentido. Ultrapassar-se mentalmente após ter feito um salto de quarenta anos num corpo que nos pertence. Mais não se reconhecer, sentir-se diminuído, vieillie e feio, pesado e deficiente. Sem saída de socorros, querer gritar a sua dor mais não viver "normalmente", urrar o seu sofrimento a ser impedido cada segundo fazer mais menor gesto, gemer a sua angústia, o seu medo do dia seguinte, a apreensão dos dias próximos, do envelhecimento brusco, a doença e a deficiência. Vomitar este golpe do destino para deixá-lo no esquecimento...

Tanto dores físicas e morais incompreendidos como nulo pode aliviar.

O meu não especialista, inicialmente reticente à cortisona, verdadeiro bálsamo para o corpo que esconde um desenvolvimento de uma perturbação qualquer, por último tem-se decidido a prescrever-o (durante quatro anos de trinta miligramas por dia o primeiro mês seguidamente vinte e cinco miligramas durante três meses, até à uma diminuição progressiva os dois últimos anos à dois miligramas). Bebidas lácteas hyperprotéinées por cura regular foram-me prescritas. Este regime alimentar foi salvador. As dores diminuíram-se claramente e o meu peso começou a estofar-se. Em seis meses, reencontrava a minha silhueta de antan. Outros carimbos contra a ansiedade, a descontração muscular, e a vitamina D foram acrescentadas. As minhas crispações musculares e tendinites permaneceram no estado, impedindo-me progredir favoravelmente e ganhar em flexibilidade. O lucro importante foi o da progressão da doença parada graças à cortisona, e a nítida diminuição da dor conservando ao mesmo tempo o estado intacto fortes contractures. Não posso ir para além meus contractures e não sinto dor. Isto foi um grande alívio para mim. Como viver este ao mesmo tempo estado doloroso na minha cabeça de quarenta anos e o corpo de uma velha senhora de noventa anos?

Onde pode vir a origem real dos meus mais? Não quero fechar-se neste círculo preto. Os anos passam e recuso ser doente. Não há. Interrogo-me durante longas horas sobre a sua origem. Quero sair da minha procura com elementos convincentes. Ao fio das minhas reflexões à investigação de coïncidentes, subo à minha infância e percursos de novo o caminho da minha vida sobre um plano médico, sentimental e profissional. Procuro as repetições, os acontecimentos notáveis, felizes ou infelizes da minha vida. Extraio na minha memória. Faço um longo trabalho de investigação sobre a minha família durante vários meses.

2.

As perturbações posturaux e físicas

Sinto-me bloqueado, endurecido, impedido por uma força sobrenatural que efetue todos os gestos simples da vida. Tomo gradualmente possessão de uma armadura à maneira de corpos. Os meus músculos e tendões inflaram, endurecidos pela inflamação muscular. Impedem qualquer movimento clássico e qualquer mobilidade. Os meus pés encontram-se então à ano-luz das minhas mãos!

1 - Perturbações posturaux

Do mais distante possível da minha memória, o meu corpo sempre foi flexível. Ao colégio ou o liceu, gostava de fazer a árvore direita ou a roda. Estirava-me frequentemente e tinha uma sensação de bem-estar neste estado. Tinha uma inclinação para o gym ao solo. No entanto, de ano em ano, endurecia-me insensivelmente, sem mesmo estar a tornar-me conta. À vinte anos, aquando do balancim antes do meu tronco para inclinar-se, pernas esticadas para atingir o solo com os meus dedos braços tensos, não chegava mais a pôr as minhas mãos ao comprido à terra. Durante uma viagem à Roma com os meus pais, à idade de vinte anos, recordo-me de um dia de degrau intenso para visitas de monumentos. Senti meus desenvolvo os músculos de endurecer-se à parte côncava dos joelhos durante a noite. À para levantar, tinha perdido qualquer mobilidade! Sentia fortes rigidezes e tinha o mal a andar rapidamente para seguir os passos da minha família. Sem dúvida, a origem é o aquecimento dos meus tendões sur-sollicitation. Aquilo traduzia-se por uma sensação dolorosa de queimadura ao degrau, sobretudo desenvolver-lo os músculos de frio.

Seguidamente cerca de anos atrasado, para tocar a ponta dos dedos ao solo pernas tensas, devia tirar sobre os meus costas desmedidamente.

Ao cerca de trinta, pratiquei a sapatilhas em equipa pessoa de hierarquia superior durante duas estações. Adorava este desporto ao colégio. Era capitão de equipa. O meu professor de Desporto tinha-me observado e mesmo tinha proposto retornar na equipa departamental. Era voluntário, rápido, e sempre em cabeça em frente da equipa adversa para marcar cestos e mobilizar os meus adversários para a vitória no entanto, asfixiava à cada travessia de terreno correndo. A minha resistência estava ao nível mínimo. Ficava vermelho escarlate no fim do jogo. Não era à vontade para correr muito simplesmente. A minha vitalidade e o meu dinamismo físico diminuiam-se.

Tomei cursos de barra ao solo à trinta e sete anos que fizeram de tomar consciência que a minha juventude afastava-se. Sentadas ao solo, pernas afastadas, gordas rigidezes dorsais impediam o meu progresso adiante. Os meus dedos tinham muita dificuldade para apanhar os meus pés! As minhas coxas endurecidas não podiam estender-se quando inclinava o meu tronco sobre cada perna. Para além do tempo que passa, encontrava-me bem bloqueado por uma força invisível que retinha-me desmedidamente.

Problema de postura

A sensação de partir sobre o lado direito andando é usual. A falta de estabilidade é flagrante. Os meus passos são ligeiros, procurando compensá-lo. A minha abóbada plantar não traz tomada ao solo certa e firme. Tenho compreendido atrasado oito anos a origem deste disfuncionamento.

2 - Perturbações corporai

O corpo

Compreender rapidamente que a impossibilidade de reduzir-me adiante ou ser acocorado, com grandes dificuldades para sentar-me e levantar-me de uma cadeira devido fortes a tensões musculares que dessensibilizem as minhas coxas feitas parte do meu diário. Dormir ao comprido ventre não é mais possível.

A subida e a descida dos degraus são complicadas de apreender, um unicamente um após o outro, como fazem-no as crianças inferior idade.

O degrau prolongado deve evitar-se porque causa crispações a nível das coxas, barrigadas perna, do pescoço e os ombros. É mesmo impossível em terreno acidentado ou mesmo seixoso.

A cozinha, a entrevista da casa (passar o aspirador, o serpillère, pressionar uma esponja, fazer as camas...), as corridas (manipulação dos artigos e o seu peso), conduzir ou ainda ocupar-me da minha vida de família com uma jovem criança à carga (cuidados diários) é um trabalho penoso e doravante fazer com precaução e lentamente.

A minha rapariga ao infantário alimenta-se normalmente à meio-dia enquanto compro produtos manufaturados para alimentar-me ao trabalho.

A parte superior do corpo

A postura altera-se a nível do pescoço endurecido afixado adiante e os ombros sem estar a poder girar parte e outra completação.

Os membros

Os meus membros são duros como piques com uma grande dificuldade para levantar os meus braços. Fechar um sutiã com os braços na costas ficou-me impossível.

Numerosos despertadores noturnos espalham as minhas noites. Dores paralisam-me os membros superiores e inferiores. Devido a posições prolongadas das pernas e braços dobrados, mais menor movimento de despregadura das minhas pernas e os meus braços luta sobre os meus músculos endurecidos assim solicitados. Qual dor! A obrigação de mover se não permanecer mim tenso à nunca acompanhado de um sentimento vivo de queimadura nos meus músculos com o meu movimento muito lento sobre as minhas articulações duras e duras. Era terrível a viver e assim doloroso.

A pele

Acrescenta-se uma pele encaixotada, seca e irritada sobre todo o corpo, mal irrigada, de uma cor azulada e marmoreada.

O rosto

Enrugar orais

Decorrem enrugar orais, largas bandas verticais em redor da boca que acentuam o envelhecimento já prematuro pela doença.

Encolhimento oral

Seguiu rapidamente com uma abertura à apenas dois centímetros e metade.

Pele estirada

Sobretudo sobre o rosto a nível do frente e a boca, étirement excessivo da pele dá forma à uma máscara inestética.

Boca

Tenho uma sensação de picadas dentro das minhas faces e sobretudo sobre a minha língua a dever eliminar o dentifrício à hortelã quando lavo-me os dentes. Mastigar uma pastilha elástica à hortelã não é desejável.

As mãos

O fenómeno mais embaraçoso é a impossibilidade de encerramento/abertura das mãos com perda de força. A condução automóvel era-me difícil mas não insuperável, a classificação de papéis, a escrita ou a introdução por teclado de documentos embaraçosos mas não proibida... A manipulação de papel é extremamente reduzida e causa rapidamente rachas. As mãos ao comprido não são mais possíveis. As articulações são vermelhas.

É suficiente imaginar uma abertura permanente das mãos com dedos quase tensos, ligeiramente encolhidos e deformados !Os talheres tornam-se difíceis ter, a faca a manipularem, os utensílios de cozinha pesados a levarem, os vidros bem demasiado largos para a minha nova morfologia... A sensibilidade da pele a nível da extremidade dos dedos é extremamente fina. Préhension é por conseguinte embaraçoso e doloroso. Sentir a sua última falange é que desabilita e invalidando.

São estreitamente ligados uma perda de força inegável e uma impossibilidade a levar do peso (um quilograma de farinha, uma caixa de conserva, uma garrafa de água, um fogão... Parapheur ao trabalho é um pesado e o seu transporte faz-se sobre os meus antebraços. Da mesma maneira que levantar a minha rapariga para levantar-o da sua cama a manhã ou após a sesta é uma operação meticulosa com os meus antebraços. Dormiu numa cama "de grande" protegida por uma barreira.

A chegada da doença Raynaud, a nível das mãos - cujo frio dessensibiliza e branqueia as extremidades obriga a ter sobre ele luvas e evitar nos supermercados seus riscam despesas e congelados.

Vestuário

A fim de evitar qualquer complicação, é habitual vestir-me diferentemente, calçar-me diferente, (sem laço), mais não pôr joias demasiado pesadas, demasiado duras sobre a pele e demasiado incómodos, e esquecer os anéis que ferem entre os dedos pela sua fricção.

Dificuldade motricité

Uma grande dificuldade para mover invadiu-me. A impressão de ser no corpo de outra obcecava-me. Identifico-me um jovem no corpo de uma velha pessoa. Meus contractures musculares generalizados conduziram à uma incapacidade a liberar-me. Não chego a ter qualquer abrandamento muscular. Desde uma dezena de ano, o meu corpo ficou estrangeiro e comporta-se ao seu modo. Não o reconheço mais. Não responde mais aos meus pedidos. Solicito-o diferentemente sem, no entanto, chegar a liberá-lo, aliviar-o, aliviá-lo. É comprimido, oprimido, e esticado. O frio acentua este fenómeno. É o meu capital, devo no entanto tomar cuidado e amimá-lo.

Prefácio acrescido: 40% da minha vida a dormir

A noite, como se tivesse-me dado-se um golpe de maça sobre o crânio, adormecia-se de um golpe, na frente tele à vinte e uma hora trinta o mais tardar. Não derrogava à esta regra. Guardava este ritmo desde a minha adolescência, fiel à este princípio. Não uma noite, pude olhar um filme na sua integralidade! As minhas lembranças de aluno trazem-me à autorização parental de olhar todas as terças-feiras noite o western à televisão sobre uma das três cadeias possível. Sistematicamente, dormia de um sono pesado e profundo e o dia seguinte manhã, reencontrava-me na minha cama, na qual o meu pai tivesse-me depositado a véspera no fim do filme. Adulto, continuava este ritual. Posso dizer que consumi filmes télévisuels! Todas as noites, mim me cestos na frente do pequeno ecrã. Os meus olhos ficavam tanto pesados que não podia lutar. O sono é mais forte que todo, levava-me na sua esteira. O cansaço crónico é uma calamidade, uma maldição, uma deficiência. Velar noite sempre foi-me muito incômodo. Esta falta de vitalidade apreendia-me basicamente da meus entranhas sem estar a poder lutar. Após desperto à vinte e duas horas trinta, após o famoso filme que teria devido ter-me em respiração, retornava muito rapidamente na minha cama levado numa noite de torpor, sem sensação de sonhado, até à manhã. À sete horas, desperto pela campainha elétrica das cigarras do meu despertador matinal, levanto-me, com o sentimento ter dormido bem. A minha necessidade vital de uma longa noite de sono representava nove à dez horas de sono. À verdade dizer, à quarenta anos, dormi quarenta e dois para - cem da minha vida!

Falta de energia

Tanto contractures e rigidezes enfraquecem o corpo. A energia solta-se nunca. A minha falta de energia era flagrante. É desprovido de qualquer vontade. A mais menor ação parece-me uma montanha a cruzar. Todo fica insuperável. O meu corpo é inadaptado ao esforço e impedido qualquer atividade.

Perda de pesos

O cansaço físico provoca o cansaço moral e amaigrissement inevitável que é bom jugular. No entanto, caí neste círculo infernal com uma perda de dez quilos. Os médicos conhecem este fenómeno mas não antecipam. O ferro fundido muscular é fonte de mais e de dificuldades físicos da qual deve-se fazer face. Meses ou mesmo anos são necessários para subir a inclinação.

Ter frio

Desde minha lembrança mais remota, sempre sofri frilosité. A minha circulação sanguínea parece perturbada. Qual sensação desagradável os timoratos é confrontada! Mais menor o ar, mesmo estival, é-me incômodo e desagradável. Transforma-me em cubo de gelo da cabeça ao pé. As minhas extremidades espessam-se instantaneamente. O meu nariz, as minhas mãos, e os meus pés estão frescos ou mesmo frios. Impossível aquecer-me sem uma espessura suplementar. Velo sempre a ter um pulôver perto de mim, das luvas finas no meu saco bem como um boné ligeiro.

No entanto, pude constatar que desde a minha inflamação muscular, meu frilosité acentuou-se claramente porque a minha circulação sanguínea é menos fluida. O inverno, espessuras sobre a minha pele e mesmo sobvestuários muito quentes não me impedem ter frias. Três espessuras não me assustam! Sou obrigada ter vinte e três graus dentro para ser confortável sendo vestida ao mesmo tempo calorosamente. À bonita estação, conservo os meu adesivos, blusão e luvas para evitar contratar-se desmedidamente. Em julho, há dois anos, surpreendi-me pôr sobvestuários quentes enquanto que os meus colegas levavam T-shirt. Mais menor vento congela-me. O Mistral que sopra mais que de costume no vale do Rhône acentua este fenómeno de frio porque, para os que conhecem-no, passa através dos vestuários e é difícil proteger-se.

Perturbações do humor

As tensões corporais provocam uma falta de controlo nas minhas reações.

Receptivo à pressão atmosférica

Por tempos chuvosos ou ventosos, o meu corpo reage de maneira desfavorável. É encarregado de íons negativos que perturbam as crispações e favorecem as rachas e a seca da pele.

A lista não é exaustiva porque o diário em geral pesa pesado e põe problemas. À cada momento, os meus gestos lentos e inábeis trazem-me à dolorosa realidade. Sou impedida. É duro da cabeça ao pé.

3 - Tratamentos médicos e cirúrgicos

Cura preventivo

Além disso, a fim de paliar aos desagrados das doenças infanteis, o pediatra tinha-nos tomado como cobaias, o meu irmão mais velho e eu mesmo em jardim de infância e primário para experimentar uma cura preventivo de injeções de gama globulina para passar o inverno. A enfermeira fazia-nos picaduras muito dolorosas nas nádegas. A dor foi a mesma coisa intensa e a sua lembrança. Os meus gritos aquando das picaduras da enfermeira, o sentimento de sofrer no constrangimento, sem estar a compreender os pseudónimos benefícios, a ausência da minha mãe que não suportava de ver e de entender e a presença imponente do meu pai pareciam-me uma tortura. Deste episódio, mim sebe as picaduras sous toutes ses formes, das tomadas de sangue à acupunctura sentir-me mal, contratar-me e mesmo ter uma indisposição quando a enfermeira se insucesso. Muito em não ser doente, estava numa espiral infernal de constrangimentos médicos dos quais ter-me-ia passado de boa vontade. A minha desconfiança junto do corpo médico era já a caminho. Provou-se que este pediatra foi suspendido das suas funções durante três anos, em fim de carreira para exercício ilícito da medicina.

Problemas orais

Testei muito jovem a experiência do dentista e das cáries. Da parte superior dos meus seis anos, as minhas cáries desenvolviam-se, um às, sobre um dente seguidamente outra, à destino de um prémolaire receptivas cujo esmalte era friável. Nos anos 70, o dentista não utilizava água com o rodízio. Das minhas lembranças de infância, girava lentamente mas procurava-me dores e tinha um odor de queimado. Não gostava do dentista. Porque cáries? No entanto, não comia bombom, nem bebia sumos açucarados. Sem dúvida que os meus dentes definitivos foram fragilizados pela absorção tétracycline, medicamento prescreve à idade de três anos para tratar da minha coqueluche. Desde cerca de anos, este medicamento é menos proibido às crianças de oito anos! Foi reconhecido que os dentes sofrem o efeito destrutivo deste antibiótico. Fragiliza os dentes por um esmalte friável sobre os dentes definitivos em preparação e tonalidade de uma coloração anormal os dentes definitivos de maneira irreversível de um cinzento mais escuro para a gengiva que se degrada de um tom mais claro para baixo. Mim sofridos já à minha jovem idade os efeitos das incoerências médicas: a saúde pública que põe sobre o mercado à destino a partir de jovens crianças dos medicamentos inadaptados. Os meus dentes de leite, brancos como pérolas, foram substituídos por dentes definitivos tentados e estriados de desagradáveis toms de cinzento degradado mais escuro para a gengiva sobre a integralidade da minha dentição.

Tentei fazer blanchissement de dentes por goteiras no meu dentista em 1995 - não reembolsado pela segurança social sobre incisivas o inferior e superior. O resultado foi convincente porque recuperei duas tonalidades mas o cinzento persiste ainda hoje em dia. O temor de tornar dentes mais os frágeis trava-me na realização de outras goteiras vinte anos após. O retrocesso não é feito sobre este tipo de sintoma contrariamente à tonalidade por bebidas (café, chá) ou cigarros.

Recomendação anódino é-me feita pelo meu dentista ao cerca de trinta sobretudo não mastigar da pastilha elástica devido gordos a amálgamas que poderiam não se opôr à pressão, de fazer salivar aumentando ao mesmo tempo o risco de fratura dental.

Grandes dificuldades para abrir a minha maxila esticam no máximo os tendões do contorno da boca para uma abertura de dois centímetros apenas. Morder uma maçã fica muito complicado e doloroso como uma queimadura.

Operação da apendicite

À idade de nove anos, fui operada de uma crise de apendicite que puxava-me desde longos meses mais a não poder andar longamente. Dia de mercado, devia fazer pausas para retornar à pé à casa. As dores abdominais tiravam-me baixo no ventre mais a não poder fazer um passo. A única solução era o descanso forçado e a posição alongada durante trinta minutos. Esta prova à clínica assim jovem não me deixa indiferente. Estreia anestesia geral com endormissement ao balão para evitar as picaduras para as quais tenho um santo horror, seguidamente o desejo irresistível de beber após o meu despertador sem ter a possibilidade, a dificuldade para andar o dia seguinte com dor abdominal, a primeira noite fora o meu cocoon familiar, num mundo hostil, acompanhada da minha peluche, um grande coelho branco tentado de bege oferecido pelos meus pais e pela lembrança de uma refeição saltada por esquecimento da enfermeira. A minha apendicite num tubo transparente era inflamada e escurecida e não muito bonito ver após a operação. A sua lembrança está muito presente ainda. A minha cicatriz é quase invisível e devo alugar as competências do cirurgião.

Afeições nasais

Sinusites, rhinites crónicos e rhinofaringites fazem o objeto do meu diário desde os anos 90. Sofri de frios, de nariz tapado à repetição sem, no entanto, apanhar frio. Consultei um especialista que indicou-me que a minha divisória nasal era deformada ligeiramente mas que nada não justificava estas repetições. Preconizou um pulverizador nasal à cada crise. Gastei das toneladas de lenços papel durante anos. O desencadeamento opera-se geralmente à primavera que poderia fazer pensar à uma origem alérgica

Queda de tensão

Esgoto-me regularmente. À cada mudança de estação, a minha tensão aproxima os nove e moscas divertem-se passar na frente dos meus olhos com dificuldades para descer as escadas e uma sensação estranha de ter as minhas pernas de algodão tal uma boneca de pano. O medo de cair sem estar a poder reter-me e quebrar-me um membro tendo em conta as suas extremas rigidezes a dobrar-se puxa-me. É o sinal de um descanso merecido bem.

Vacinação ao modo

Devi proteger-me das doenças. As vacinas tiveram a parte bonita sobre o meu corpo contra as doenças infanteis. Testei também à trinta anos a vacina da hepatite B parado em cursos de tratamento (três tomadas) tendo em conta os efeitos secundários desacreditados pela opinião pública.

Três meses antes da minha inflamação muscular, tive a vacina do DT paralisia infantil. Conhece-se as interrogações mitigadas sobre as consequências nefastas das vacinas sobre o corpo humano e o desencadeamento de doenças. Coincidência ou não?

Problemas de pele

Rapidamente, fortes contractures, a limitação dos movimentos e a falta de desporto reduziram a circulação sanguínea que causa problemas de pele a nível das mãos com rachas e a hipersensibilidade das extremidades dos dedos. A seca a nível das mãos é importante. A pele é encaixotada a nível dos antebraços. A cor é azulada. Comichões parecem aliviar a seca perto dos pulsos. As articulações são vermelhas. Os dedos a nível das falanges e as articulações são inflados. As cutículas são inexistentes. Certas unhas são estriados. As unhas são quase brancas com os dedos tensos. As falanges são vermelhas.

Nenhum dermatologista, não especialista, ou farmacêutico pôde trazer-me uma solução eficaz para o alívio da seca a nível da palma das mãos e sobretudo os dedos. Fico testeuse de todas as natas postas sobre o mercado! Além disso, pequenos botões têm aparecido nas palmas das mãos ocasionalmente.

O meu corpo apresenta igualmente sinais de seca sobre as pernas (sobretudo as barrigadas perna e os.pés) e os braços.

Em 2011, os meus problemas de pele a nível das mãos me insupportent. Desde quatro longos anos não vejo melhoria. Espero cerca de conselhos por um outro corpo médico. Excepcionalmente, o dermatologista, chefe de serviço do hospital, atribui-me uma hospitalização de dia sobre dois dias perto do meu lugar de habitação para cerca de exames médicos. Direção o oftalmologista que, após um fundo do olho e uma tortura para ver o estado dos meus olhos e considerar se um medicamento (com efeito secundário: uma infração ocular) poderia mim ser prescreve. O medicamento é abandonado devido ao estado pouco avançado da doença. A tortura ocular teria podido ser evitada!

Infração pulmonaa

Em 2011, único uma pequena infração pulmonaa alveolar é descobertos. Exames sobre a minha capacidade pulmonaa são realizados e confirmados uma restrição respiratória de 30% em relação à uma mulher da minha idade. A fibrose pulmonaa deve supervisionar-se cada ano. Terá sido necessário de esperar cinco anos para fazer este exame e esta constatação!

Problema de imunidade

Fala-se também da doença autoimune: a síndrome de sobreposição sclérodermie e o dermatomyosite tendo em conta os sintomas físicos.

Os anticorpos antinucleares 1/800 e anti PMScl são positivo este ano, ou seja cinco anos após a inflamação muscular. O corpo médico põe por último um nome sobre a doença: sclérodermie. Faz parte das doenças órfãs (uma fraca parte da população é atingida) embora espalhe-se cada vez mais junto das mulheres hoje em dia.

É verdadeiro que conhecer qual afeição sofre-se, alivia o nosso mental. Conhece-se melhor à qual esperar-se. Neste caso, trata-se de uma patologia pouco larga. Pode atacar os órgãos vitais que não é o meu caso. É justa à primeira fase e não evoluiu desde dez anos. Aquilo incentiva-me fortemente ganhar de dia em dia o combate contra ela.

Aparecimento de nódulos

Em 2011, após o fim da tomada de cortisona, dos nódulos sob cutâneos apareceu sobre as minhas articulações dos cotovelos e os joelhos sobretudo. A impossibilidade de fazer uma cobrança pelo dermatologista tendo em conta a fixação aos tendões não permitiu de determinar a sua composição porque invisíveis à rádio (enquanto que teriam podido ser da calcificação).

4 - Qualidade de vida deteriorada

A minha vida em geral foi perturbada por todos os incumprimentos e todas as dificuldades que se traduziu por uma nítida diminuição dos meus desempenhos físicos. O mínimo vital era necessário e o descanso necessário à cada momento de liberdade fora do quadro profissional.

Perdi a autonomia ao sentido limpo do termo ou seja a viabilidade de executar uma tarefa qualquer com facilidade. Grandes dificuldades com perda de marcadores mergulharam-me na sequência da minha inflamação muscular profunda numa desordem que não pode ser compreendida pelo comum do mortais se não for o que vive esta situação ao idêntico. Todo parece-me insuperável.

Grandes dificuldades para utilizar as minhas mãos retraídas diariamente retardam-me na integralidade dos meus movimentos e retornam-me uma imagem degradada, envelhecida e insuportável da minha limpa pessoa. Tomei vinte, ou mesmo cinquenta anos de um golpe! Encontro-me num corpo de uma pessoa da quarta idade (e ainda, muito entre são mais alertas que mim) conservando ao mesmo tempo a minha juventude mental dos meus quarenta anos.

Sofro no meu corpo duro como um robô, encarcerado numa armadura, sem mesmo poder estirar-se. O diário torna-se rapidamente uma fonte de frustrações.

Perda de autonomia nas atividades domésticas

Sinto-me cativo do meu corpo. Perco os meus marcadores. Tenho tanto dificuldades para fazer que gerir a casa, a cozinha (descascar, cortar, levar os utensílios de cozinha) e a entrevista (vassoura, serapilheira, poeira) é muito complicada e executada com dor e queimaduras.

Perda de autonomia nas atividades sociais e de lazeres O desejo soltou-se de sair nmim porque todo parece-me insuperável. Apreendo o único facto de mover o meu corpo! Os lazeres passam doravante ao segundo plano. Ao trabalho, a dor é acrescentada o meu gestuelle lento e difícil. Constantemente sou impedida nos meus movimentos mais simples do diário: tomar a combinação do telefone, girar as páginas de um processo, escrever, sentar-me, levantar-me, reduzir-me, recuperar um objeto ao solo, etc.

Perda de autonomia em família

A minha dificuldade para ocupar-me da minha rapariga inferior idade no entanto deu-me a força de superar as minhas dificuldades, obrigada criar-o e responder às suas necessidades. Isto permitiu-me -me não ankyloser e de desenvolver mais força sobre a minha mão direita porque é destro.

Perda de autonomia nos cuidados pessoais

A primeira dificuldade é tomar um banho. A posição sentada ao solo é-me impossível menos à de deixar-me cair sobre as nádegas. Mas como fazer para aumentar-me com as minhas mãos na forma de gancho, sem força e sem mobilidade? Tomar o chuveiro na banheira é um calvário porque difícil de acessos sem estar a poder levantar os postes que me servem de pernas. Estabilizar-se seguidamente sobre um solo que desliza aumenta da proeza. Muitas precauções e de tempos são necessárias.

Que este-o escondido é baixo! Os meus pés são bem distante das minhas mãos! Qual dificuldade para calçar-me, pôr adesivos ou meias, para cortar-me as unhas e pôr-me do verniz, e mesmo para lavar-me os pés!

A costas são igualmente uma zona difícil de acessos. Que dizer do meu rosto que nunca não pareceu ser também ósseo com os meus dedos aduncos que não podem apreender-o facilmente. Estender uma nata pelo corpo da extremidade dos dedos - com dor na torção do pulso e rigidezes nos dedos é rico de ensinos.

<h1 style="text-align:center">3.</h1>

<h1 style="text-align:center">As perturbações digestivas</h1>

Vômitos à repetição

Desde a minha mais jovem idade, frequentemente tive crises de fígado e crises de acetona até à adolescência. A minha especialidade era o vômito contra a minha vontade! Lembranças mal a ser devidas aos mais de ventre, de amargura na boca, de queimadura no estômago, de cansaço... retornam. Os transportes acentuavam este fenómeno. Seguidamente veio o período das gastroenterites à repetição cada ano durante uma vintena de anos.

Ventre inflado intempestivo

Desde a minha mais terna infância, sofria ballonnements à repetição. É o sintoma que caracteriza-me mais. Pode-se imaginar-se uma pequena rapariga com um ventre inflado como baudruche! Fragilizados pelos as bebidas gasosas, os lacticínios e pela farinha de trigo, meus intestinos faziam-se a parte bonita a mostrar a sua existência ao comum do mortais. A vergonha atenazava-me. Ao mar, com o meu fato duas peças, e a minha silhueta fina e élancée, arvorava um ventre redondo bem tenso como os biafranos do terceiro mundo na África. Os meus fatos limitavam-se à dimensões acima a minha, (um à dois) dos vestuários largos, amplos para esconder as minhas inflações repetitivas. Tentei mesmo à vinte anos os vestuários de gravidez com uma cuecas que, resolutamente, não era adaptada à minha morfologia fina.

Estes ballonnements tomavam-me à qualquer hora do dia, sem estar a prevenir acompanhados de dores geralmente antes de trinta anos e importantes desordens intestinais após esta idade. Frequentemente rapidamente após a refeição, com um prato de massas ao bolognaise, alimentos crus, um consumo de pão industrial, de leite, bebidas gasosas, etc. era um colecionador de colites e ballonnements. O incómodo estava lá. Muito tempo tenho pensado que a alimentação cru era responsável. Era o meu segundo cérebro! Reagia sem nula dúvida à pressão diária, demasiado forte engulir pelo meu verdadeiro cérebro. Hipersensível e secreto, tinha o mal a esconder as minhas emoções através do meu ventre. Inflava-se de ar, como para dizer-me que tinha fartar-se de rir. Ao fio dos anos, devia suportar avalement de qualquer alimento em refeições expressar, o stress do trabalho, a vida que trepida da corrida boulot-dodo. Refletia ao meu lugar... Tanto falsas desculpas que não davam nenhuma melhoria quanto suas a supressão na minha vida corrente.

Os meus problemas de colites nunca foram diagnosticados por um médico não especialista e especialista. Nenhum medicamento específico nem nenhum conselho foi-me dado para remediar. Consultei um médico não especialista não conventionné nos anos 2000 que falou-me pela primeira vez de probiotiques consumir em cura. Graças sua a absorção, a melhoria fez-se de sentir no meu organismo sem, no entanto, evacuar os inconvenientes menos frequentes.

No entanto, recentemente quase eliminei o leite e os seus derivados e reduzo o meu consumo em glúten (produtos manufaturados, pão, produtos açucarados...) O meu conforto digestivo melhorou-se inevitavelmente sem, no entanto, de maneira espetacular.

4.

As perturbações cognitivas

1 - Baixa de desempenhos intelectuais

O peso da doença provoca a baixa de todas as capacidades nomeadamente intelectuais. O mental não segue mais porque obcecado pelo mal e apresentado à isolamento. O cérebro é amaciado calcificado, esvaziado. Passei concursos administrativos durante numerosos anos sem ter um resultado suficientemente positivo apesar das minhas competências profissionais e o meu nível de estudos. Tenho a impressão de ser ao lado dos meus sapatos.

Perda de memória

Tenho uma facilidade de aprendizagem e uma boa memória desde os meus jovens anos escolares. A minha memória visual ajuda-me muito. Ora, para além do peso das idades que limita a memória, pude constatar certa dificuldade para memorizar.

Dificuldade de atenção

A minha concentração à cada momento sobre o meu mal ao despertador de cada dor mim impedido ter uma concentração contínua. Vivo o meu mal à cada segundo autocarro ele recordo-me sistematicamente à sua lembrança.

2 - Domínio das emoções e a sensibilidade

Ansiedade: A confrontação da doença num futuro incerto preocupa o nosso inconsciente e gasta o nosso diário. As dores físicas adicionam-se às dores morais e formam um cocktail que fragiliza-nos. Os médicos podem tratar apenas por anxiolytiques - boia de socorros provisória até mesmo prescrevem antidepressivo que aliviam apenas sintomas e mascaram a realidade. A vida é insuportável no sofrimento mas é-o na mesma proporção ao meu sentido que viver-o com antidepressivo.

A percepção

A simples vista de um objeto pesado ou difícil de manipulação (como a rolha de uma caneta ou uma garrafa de água) ou ainda o volume de carga a efetuar (como a triagem de papéis, o facto de folhear uma revista...) perturba-me com o medo não lá de não chegar e dever gastar da força física que perdi.

Hipersensibilidade

Pude constatar o desenvolvimento da minha hipersensibilidade. Estou mais à escuta do meu corpo e é por conseguinte mais receptivo à qualquer sinal. Por exemplo, sinto circular as energias nas minhas pernas aquando de sessões de acupunctura e de magnetismo. A minha hipersensibilidade aumentouse consideravelmente desde estes últimos anos.

Ímã sensibilidade às ondas

Certas joias (em mesmo ouro), os relógios, os apoios abarrota à reforço metálico e os óculos de metal causam-me uma sensibilidade eletromagnética que se manifesta por perturbações neurológicas. A sensibilidade às ondas eletromagnéticas é aumentada quando mim útil o meu computador portátil sobre os meus joelhos. Tenho então o mal a levantar-me devido fortes a rigidezes musculares nas barrigadas perna e a nível dos joelhos. As minhas mãos são crispadas. Ao escritório, sinto o escritório metálico condutor das ondas e as sensações desagradáveis de vibrações nas minhas pernas.

Segunda parte

Os confortos de vida

O caos passado e estes meses "de zombie", na pele de outra, desperto com a firme vontade de sair-se. Podia convencer-se apenas mim era doente. Não merecia aquilo. Sempre tinha tido uma vida calma e sã sem excessos. O que por conseguinte teria desencadeado esta doença?

1.

A vertente médica

1 – a medicina allopathique

Nunca tive grande confiança ao corpo médico. À cinco anos, o único pediatra, preconizava um regime à base de picaduras mês à base gammaglobuline a fim de prevenir as doenças infanteis extremamente dolorosa. Este tratamento no entanto não foi eficaz dado que o meu irmão e eu mesmo são atingidos de doença autoimune. O traumatismo das picaduras permanece intacto ainda e gravado na minha memória. Apreendo a mais menor agulha e as tomadas de sangue são para mim um calvário. Mim endurecidos qualquer meu corpo à vista de uma simples agulha. Para tanto, procuro desesperadamente certo conforto de vida para aligeirar as minhas rigidezes.

Vacinação

A modificação de procedimento de vacinação da hepatite B pelos poderes públicos interroga-me ainda. Alguns atribuem-se a dizer que o alumínio nas vacinas poderia perturbar a imunidade e desenvolver doenças autoimunes. Mas o benefício das vacinas mais importantes que os eventuais problemas, as vacinas permanecem sobre o mercado.

A vacinação do DT Paralisia infantil três meses antes da minha inflamação muscular torna-me perplexos ainda que os médicos concedem-se dizer que o retrocesso é suficientemente grande para açoitar-o.

Sessões de fisioterapia

Três sessões de fisioterapeuta por semana trazem ao meu corpo os benefícios de flexibilidade e de bem-estar a nível do do pescoço, a costas, as pernas e as mãos. Da drenagem linfática dos membros inferiores e superiores dão-me um sentimento de ligeireza nos meus braços e as minhas pernas. Testei numerosos fisioterapeutas. Alguns são girados para o abrandamento e o abrandamento com massagens suaves, outros fazem massagens úteis (mãos, pés, costass). O benefício está sempre presente.

Controlos médicos hospitalares

A fim de melhorar o meu diário, girei-me para o Centro hospitalar universitário em 2011 para ser seguida regularmente pelos mesmos pessoais e materiais idênticos.

Exames foram efetuados e pôde ser realizado um acompanhamento médico anual. Nenhuma evolução desfavorável desde 2011. Contudo, o sentimento de ser objeto de curiosidade durante as consultas dos internos e visitas de estudantes é bastante forte e antes ruim na frente do olhar vazio do pessoal médico e a ausência de comentário.

Ao longo dos anos desde a inflamação muscular, foi-me indicado pelo corpo médico as doenças sucessivas seguintes: o fibromyalgie, o dermatomyosite, a síndrome de sobreposição sclérodermie e dermatomyosite seguidamente sclérodermie na sequência do indicador positivo dos anticorpos. É dizer que o diagnóstico foi incerto durante cinco anos, período durante o qual fiz apenas tomadas de sangue regulares.

Ergoterapeuta

O meu encontro com o ergoterapeuta do hospital pôs-me do bálsamo ao coração graças seu a otimismo e as suas competências. Grande mulher morena frisado ao olhar vivo que combina as suas competências profissionais à sua empatia, o seu sentido da comunicação e o seu bom humor. A cada um das minhas sessões, ganho cerca de milímetros na abertura e o encerramento das minhas mãos. Trabalha sobre as fáscias que são finas membranas que envolvem os músculos e órgãos que se contratam nomeadamente sobre crispações, o stress e procura massagens manuais que facilitam o trabalho de descontração dos tendões. Ajudada de ferramentas eficientes, faz-me trabalhar três horas por dia durante uma semana. O mental deve habituar-se a ganhar em flexibilidade e reencontrar posturas que não integra mais. O trabalho por momento dá a impressão que os dedos vão quebrar-se devido à apreensão e da dor mas o lucro é certo: um meiocentímetro por dedo por semana. As sessões são fatigantes mas tanto benéficas. Para tanto, o trabalho faz-se em doçura, com massagens e da manipulação adequada à patologia. Ganhei três centímetros por dedo ao encerramento graças seu a intervenção em quatro curas. O meu objetivo permanece o encerramento total das minhas mãos. A amplitude articulaa não atingida, a esperança não é uma astúcia. O inconveniente do ofício é a sua tomada de acordo com regras estritas de hospitalização à razão de dois à três vezes por ano. A ergoterapia é útil à melhoria dos sintomas ou mesmo a sua cura. Esta especialidade não é desenvolvida bastante no nosso país.

2 - As medicinas alternativas e paralelas

Os benefícios da ioga e sophrologie

Pratiquei durante dois anos acelerei-o ioga nos anos 80, ensinada por uma mulher de experiência.Os movimentos lentos e aplicados de flexibilidade e étirement, manutenção e força trazem um bem-estar físico e mental, um abrandamento e uma plenitude confortáveis bem como um tónus corporais. Esta prática física completa diária de uma hora trinta minutos traz tal abrandamento mental que põe-se em lugar uma atitude zen que dura cerca de dias ou mesmo a semana. Muitos benefícios são reconhecidos nesta técnica vinda da Índia. Mas desde os meus problemas de saúde, é-me impossível pôr-me ao solo. Contudo, pratico a respiração abdominal a fim de aliviar-se.

A análise da genealogia

Aquilo foi a ocasião de fazer investigações sobre a minha genealogia e construir a minha árvore genealógica a fim de compreender a minha história familiar. Convido mesmo os meus antepassados ao meu percurso para encontrar as relações entre os seres e as suas semelhanças. Ajudado das datas de nascimento dos meus antepassados e o seu percurso de vida, fiz descobertas interessantes. Anoto critérios genéticos, identificações, semelhanças, uma fidelidade familiar, etc. chego gradualmente a fazer relações. Desenham-se então sobre a minha pálete alegre os traços estruturados da minha história programada.

As sessões de kinésiologie

O kinésiologue, antiga enfermeira, pratica o kinésiologie, com várias técnicas desde longos anos. Alongado sobre uma cama, deixo-me ir ao abrandamento. Utiliza o pêndulo, as pedras, os óleos essenciais, os mapas das plantas. Interroga o espaço tempo (presente, passado, futuro) com o pêndulo a fim de partir à investigação de um disfuncionamento eventual.

Fez de surgir as minhas fraquezas, os meus medos e as minhas interrogações. Falei-lhe dos meus bloqueios profissionais. Permitiu-me pôr uma imagem positiva sobre eu mesmo para seguir em frente. A partir da primeira sessão, pude constatar o benefício do trabalho sobre as energias porque tomei consciência das minhas competências de escritor e o resultado do meu projeto de escrita de livro uma dezena de dias após. Então criei a minha estrutura de escritor público Plum' issime. Pediu-me que pusesse uma imagem precisa de planta nos meus lugares de passagem a fim de ter-o à vista geralmente possível. Chegado ao meu domicílio, tomei os meus pinceis e tenho pinto a imagem florescida. Esta primeira sessão foi muito frutuosa porque desenvolveu a minha criatividade. Duas outras sessões seguiram. O kinésiologue foi surpreendido ao mesmo tempo e deleitado do benefício das suas ações. Indicou-me que permanecerei nos seus anais.

O magnetismo

Testado cerca de quinze anos anteriormente para problemas de excesso de trabalho profissional e de cansaço, girei-me para um magnétiseur. Saio destas sessões com uma energia e um abrandamento que me fazem muito bem. Há para recarregar-me em energia e para aliviar as minhas tensões. É muito satisfeito desta prática.

A descoberta da acupunctura

Igualmente girei-me para a acupunctura que me permitia fazer circular as energias no meu corpo. À cada sessão semanal, as agulhas plantadas a costas, nos ombros, a cimeira do crânio e as orelhas perfuravam o meu corpo cuja pele fina sentia geralmente as picaduras como agressões físicas. Um mal para um bem porque nas minhas barrigadas perna circulava uma onda inteira de ebulição, tal uma torrente.

A descoberta da homeopatia

Sou-me decidida consultar um homeopata para um trabalho de fundo, sobre o terreno imune. Um homeopata incita-me mais investir-se num tratamento a longo prazo porque o número de doses é reduzido só um um tratamento ao mesmo tempo contra diferentes tubos com um homeopata clássico. Mas a notoriedade do homeopata a clássica inclinou na balança. O tratamento homeopático a longo prazo e um tratamento de prevenção anti grippal foram-me dados.

Recentemente, fui de consultar um homeopata na minha região retiro as alergias. Dotado de pequenas garrafas que contêm os alérgenos, deposita cada garrafa seleccionada sobre o meu pescoço (sendo alongado ao mesmo tempo) seguidamente, por uma simples pressão a nível das têmporas, ele testa a alergia. Seguidamente, sem contacto físico, suprime o problema. Encontrou-me uma alergia o ao chumbo, o mercúrio, o BCG e o arsénico. Devi constatar que a minha tosse gorda matinal atenuou-se claramente a partir do dia seguinte. Por ocasião da minha segunda consulta, na sequência dépose da minha última coroa, encontrou-me uma alergia o o o ao mercúrio, o o o chumbo, os aos fenos e poeiras, as alergias ambientais, a vacina ROR e os raios gama. Duas vezes, deveu testar o mercúrio e o chumbo que parecem bem ancorado ao mais profundo dos meus órgãos. Senti os efeitos imediatos nas minhas pernas ao momento onde a garrafa é depositada sobre o meu pescoço. Raras são as pessoas que percebem esta sensibilidade. Acrescentou outro produz sem estar a revelar-me o nome a fim de constatar os efeitos. Senti picadas dos pés à cabeça, como uma corrente que me percorria todo o corpo com estremecimentos por momentos quando a pressão é demasiado forte, seguidamente uma pressão forte sobre o crânio (à base e a cimeira da cabeça sobretudo), para seguidamente escapar-se pelo sétimo chakra.

O benefício sobre a tosse é ainda mais flagrante e a seca das mãos melhorou-se.

A descoberta da osteopatia

Após o nascimento da minha rapariga, sessões de osteopatia trouxeram-me um conforto apreciável porque o meu corpo não era no seu eixo. A minha bacia verrumava adiante à direita. Em posição de pé, o meu corpo inclina sobre antes dos meus pés. Os meus dedos do pé suportam assim a integralidade do peso. A minha bacia parte adiante, os meus costas escavam-se, os meus ombros abobadam-se ligeiramente e o meu pescoço compensa a posição de trás. A correção do osteopata à cada um das minhas visitas traz-me uma ligeireza corporal que faz bem ao corpo e a moral.

O abrandamento pelo calor e as massagens

Comecei das sessões de massagem sobre o meu corpo mortificado por tanto tensões musculares. As minhas rigidezes não podiam suportar nenhum desvio como passeio à pé prolongado, corrida à pé, bicicleta, ioga e sophrologie (impossível pôr-me à terra), piscina (drenagem prematura da pele e sobretudo as mãos com rachas)... Um pouco de doçura sobre a minha pele revela-se ter um efeito que relaxa, baseado, liberando, e mesmo décongestionnant. Cerca de minutos de bem-estar contra horas de tensões! A massagem às pedras quentes facilitou meu aumentar físico em frente de meses de esgotamento e de dor. O meu orçamento agrava-se de sessões de massagens em diferentes lugares.

Além disso tomei uma assinatura para sessões semanais balnéothérapie (hammam, sauna e jacuzzi). Esta sessão de uma hora traz-me um bem louco. O calor mim convem perfeitamente. O abrandamento trazido por este tipo de técnica seguida de um chá procura-me uma felicidade total.

Réflexologie plantar

Várias vezes, beneficiei dos benefícios de massagens plantares. Os pontos de acupunctura, os meridianos e os centros das nossas energias sobre a superfície do pé ajudam a circulação a propagar-se em todo o corpo. O resultado é surpreendente. Um total abrandamento envolve-nos, o pé é ligeiro e o degrau flexível.

3 - Melhoria da minha alimentação

Tendo em conta as perturbações intestinais e ballonnements, girei-me para uma mudança de alimentação desde um ano.

A farinha de trigo

A farinha de trigo evoluiu em detrimento da sua qualidade. Ingurgitation de glúten no corpo vai contra o bem-estar digestivo. É importante interrogar-se sobre a necessidade de comer pão ou pratos cozinhados. Tenho para a minha parte suprimido mais a grande parte dos alimentos à base de farinha de trigo e os meus intestinos sentem-se muito melhor.

Os lacticínios

Testei a alimentação sem os lacticínios. Parei beber leite chocolatado que causam-me ballonnements. Evitei os iogurtes durante cerca de meses. Pude constatar um emagrecimento ao nível abdominal e um conforto digestivo. É verdadeiro que nos anos 70, os iogurtes vendiam-se à unidade num recipiente de vidro. Hoje, o comércio à grandes escalas transformou o consumo de iogurte em detrimento da qualidade nutritiva.

A investigação da defesa da imunidade

No ano 2005, fez o encontro de um não especialista fora de nomenclatura que preconizava o probiotiques. Ainda ignorados à época, no entanto segui os seus conselhos. Fiz curas durante meses a fim de melhorar o meu trânsito e reencontrar de bons intestinos.

Recentemente, sobre os conselhos de uma farmacêutica, dirigi-me para um médico não especialista que, através de análises biológicas muito detalhadas realizadas em Bélgica.

Um mês após, os resultados fora de normas são apreendidos no software adequado do médico que conclui a um tratamento homeopático a encomendar num laboratório especializado na Bélgica. O tratamento a longo prazo consiste em doses à 1000K e misturas de grânulos específicos a diluir numa pequena garrafa de água com tomada diária de uma pequena colher giratória.

Remédio da extremidade do mundo: as plantas medicinais

A minha viagem à Londres este verão conduziu-me numa rua do bairro roque punk. Um fronteamento de loja interpelou-me. Um cartaz chamava o transeunte: "Mostram a vossa língua e um médico feito um diagnóstico gratuito." Livros a venderem numa sala, plantas em outra e do chá, e o acolhimento com o médico chinês confortou-me na seriedade da sua diligência. Ousei entrar. Expliquei em inglês o objeto da minha vinda e o médico, após ter olhado a minha língua e ter tomado o meu pulso, fez-me uma prescrição sobre um cocktail de plantas para estimular a imunidade, de dar da vitalidade e de abrandar os músculos. Devo dizer que os efeitos são muito rápidos. Senti-me muito rapidamente diferente. O meu corpo abrandou-se, permitindo movimentos mais amplos, e mais flexíveis. As minhas pernas dobram-se de maneira confortável e ganho dia após dia cerca de milímetros de encerramento. Gradualmente, chego a reduzir-me, me acocorar-se e manter a posição cada vez mais. É distante o tempo onde o meu corpo permanecia duro como "um I"! A composição, à base de plantas chinesas sob a forma de cápsulas, deve encomendar-se à Londres ou em outros países. Planta mais utilizada na composição é a angélica, planta imune que sobreviveu à área glaciaire, há dezoito mil anos. Utilizado pelo os Gregos, os Hebreus e os Romanos, seu óleo essencial servia a abrandar os músculos antes dos combates e suportar melhor os golpes. Tem grandes propriedades. Utiliza-o-se para tratar as bronquites, os problemas de circulação, os espasmos musculares, os reumatismos, a insónia, a falta de energia, a inflamação dos intestinos e as indigestões. É um potente limpador sanguíneo.

2.

Os conselhos e astúcias

Pior na doença é deixar-se tomar em carga pela medicina, de pôr-se ao lugar "do paciente" e de deixar-se guiar pelo médico sem nada fazer. Porque a doença guia os nossos passos. É fácil retornar nas suas chinelas e esperar melhores dias. Esta atitude passiva em frente da vida é prejudicial para a sobrevivência. Os conselhos do não especialista são raros a fim de melhorar a sua higiene de vida pela medicina.

A fim de conservar uma autonomia relativa, a investigação da funcionalidade é necessária para ter um máximo de conforto, segurança e eficácia nos seus gestos. Para pôr todas as possibilidades de cura do seu lado, é importante ser ativo, parar fumar e ter uma alimentação equilibrada.

1 – Alimentação

Entregar em causa os seus hábitos alimentares passa pelo facto de ser prontos para limitar o seu consumo de alimentos ou de bebidas açucarados (cereais refinados, bebidas gasosas, biscoitos, pratos preparados, bombons, os produtos transformados...), pensar comer produtos locais, os legumes frescos (verdes e alegres) e os frutos vermelhos e pretos evitando as cozeduras à elevada temperatura (churrasco e frituras), e otimizar os contributos ómega 3, antioxidante, oligo-éléments, em magnésio e vitaminas C e D (anti dor e ativador do sistema imune).

A alimentação sem lacticínio e/ou sem glúten pode trazer um conforto e uma baixa das perturbações corporais.

Girar-se para herboristerie é uma condição muito interessante para aliviar os seus mais.

2 - Arranjo

Material

Evitar preferivelmente os arranjos demasiado baixos ou demasiado elevados e privilegiar antes o arranjo à altura de homem.

Utilizar armários murais à gavetas coulissants com abertura e encerramento facilitados ou armário à estantes com fraca profundidade tipo biblioteca (30 cm apenas) para acesso livre sem ter a reduzir-se para tomar um artigo basicamente do armário.

Comprar um meioarmário à sapatos com dobra de fraca profundidade (10 cm) muito fácil de utilização sem esforço para arranjar os seus sapatos.

Instalar um rehausseur à cada pé de cama, poltrona, ou sofá para trazer um pouco de altura à artigos que são baixos.

Utilizar um plano de trabalho de 95 cm de altura mínimo a fim de evitar forçar sobre toda a parte superior do corpo (pescoço, ombros, costass).

Instalar uma mesa de bar elevada na cozinha que serve de serviço, mesa de trabalho e mesa de refeições sem ter a reduzir-se.

Escolher cadeiras com bases confortáveis preferivelmente elevado para evitar sede dobrar- pernas.

Fazer instalar toilet mais elevados que a normal.

Utilizar uma prateleira antes que um computador porque o ecrã táctil é funcional.

Utensílios de cozinha

Comprar utensílios à larga manga para ter uma melhor tomada.

Utilizar facas de cerâmica cuja lâmina é mais cortante.

Habituar-se a manipular com instrumentos úteis à pilhas como abre-caixa, abre-frasco, abre-garrafa, saca-rolha, bandolim, moinho à pimenta e sal, descasca-legume que são fáceis de utilização e sobretudo que evitam forçar. A abrir-garrafa é um companheiro de vida desde vários anos, da mesma maneira que descasca-o-legume à pilhas que economizam a minha força.

A útil ruptura lâmpadas em venda em farmácia facilita a vida.

Optar pela limpeza pelo papel descartável com as caixas de lenços de papel para limpar ou mesmo os rolos de papel com distribuidor.

Comprar um arranja-chávena suspendidos pôr sobre o plano de trabalho que é à alcance de mãos.

Corridas

Servir-se de um saco à rodízios (ou caddie) para levar as corridas (qual que difícil levar demasiado pesado a nível do pulso e o braço que suportam uma parte do peso. Escolher uma caddie à três rodízios a fim de montar as escadas.

Levar preferivelmente os sacos de corrida ou outro objeto com sacos à asas largos a levarem em redor dos pulsos ou sobre os antebraços e mesmo sobre os ombros.

Limpeza

Utilizar uma vassoura vapor para o solo, as vidraças, robinetteries, tomar um duche-o e a banheira, o lavabo e a pia bem como uma vassoura para limpar o pó do solo com toalhete à uso único e uma pequena manga para os móveis.

Utilizar gelos tomar um duche à frasco bombeia ou melhor ainda do sabão
Pôr luvas de cirurgião para lavar-se os cabelos, fazer a louça ou todas as tarefas domésticas incluindo na manipulação que protege a pele e diminui a sensibilidade.

3 – Vestuário

Privilegiar as caneleiras ao adesivos. Alguns, raspado dentro para o inverno que protege efectivamente frio.

Escolher meias ou partes inferiores de contenção para a circulação sanguínea (evitar os adesivos difíceis pôr).

Comprar luvas quentes e delicados em seda (sobluvas) ou lã.

Privilegiar sobvestuários quentes especializados na proteção do frio à destino a partir de pessoas timoratas ou lugares frias. (Adesivos, T-shirt, caraco, etc.).

Escolher vestuários de cor que têm uma incidência sobre o moral. Sair do indémodable preto o inverno para decorar de cores quentes ou frias.

Suprimir os reforços nos vestuários (sutiã sobretudo).

Evitar o porto de joias aço que são condutor de ondas eletromagnéticas. Mais a grande atenção deve ser levada à certas joias de ouro que podem comportar uma mistura de vários metais igualmente condutores de ondas.

Privilegiar sapatos abertos (tipo mulos). Não utilizar encerramentos à anel nem laços nem chutam-o enfiar nem os chinelos que são difíceis de enfiar. Preferivelmente, tomar sapatos com encerramento relâmpago qual que difícil manipular. As sabrinas são fáceis de utilização. Os botins flexíveis moutonnées são muito agradáveis de levar ainda que não têm efectivamente o pé. As em acrílico estão quentes e não apertadas. Uma sola dentro pode ajudar a ter mais quente se a sola não for bastante isolante do solo.

O prato deve privilegiar-se ou na falta disso, um pequeno tacão (4 cm máximo) preferivelmente em crepe que amortece os choques e dos tacões compensados para uma melhor manutenção e evitar as quedas ou os desequilíbrios.

Braseiras nos bolsos isolam do frio as mãos e os pés. Uma pomada labial gorda para os lábios evita as fissuras ou cieiros.

4 - Cuidados do corpo

Um ponto específico pode ser encarado para amaciar as suas perturbações por cuidados do corpo: balnéothérapie (efeito antálgico e relaxando a água quente, favorece o abrandamento muscular), massagens dois à três vezes por semana na fisioterapia e modelages.

Natas adaptadas ao corpo são difíceis de encontrar. O hospital propõe uma preparação e uma nata ao ácido hialurónico reembolsado pela segurança social. Certos pensos para os dedos também são reembolsados.

Utilizar uma edredão antes que dos panos e coberturas, mais fácil de manipulação. Em inverno, o tecido de flanela traz muito calor ou de doçura.

5 - Ergonomia ao trabalho

Comprar canetas espessas ou bolas a deslizarem em redor da caneta, um agrafador à pilhas, as dedeiras borracha à farpas para escolher o papel, um braço de telefone, uma prateleira à rodízios, uma reinstalação-cotovelo, das luvas chauffants USB, um tapete que aquece, um pequeno rato, um reinstalação-pé... Pensar a pôr luvas finas de seda por exemplo para diminuir a sensibilidade dos dedos.

6 - Desenvolver a sua rede social

Aprender a respirar profundamente, praticar uma atividade física, tomar o ar para oxigenar os tecidos e aumentar a sua taxa de vitamina D, e arejar-se contribuem o melhor possível ser (para a física e o moral).

Um aspecto importante a não negligenciar é manter a rede de amigos, a família e ter atividades sociais, artísticas ou espiritualas.

7 - Tomada em conta da deficiência

A lei sobre a deficiência de 2005 para a igualdade dos direitos e as possibilidades, a participação e a cidadania das pessoas deficientes recorda os seus direitos fundamentais e a obrigação de solidariedade do conjunto da sociedade no seu favor.

Reconhecimento trabalhador deficiente

Sem acórdão de trabalho para doença durante três anos, a mutação sobre um posto à quarenta quilómetros nmim em 2009 causou uma ruptura profissional de seis meses (gerado por cansaço suplementar e dores físicas das mãos a toda a parte superior do corpo). Em paralelo, depositei um processo de declaração de trabalhador desabilitado junto da Casa departamental das pessoas deficientes (MDPH) a fim de obter uma prioridade de mutação. Este reconhecimento é igualmente útil para a reforma, para os cheques feriados (reembolso mais vantajoso). Permite também beneficiar de um terceiro tempo para os exames e concursos e constituir um processo de prestação da deficiência com o propósito de ordenamento do seu lugar de habitação, o seu lugar de trabalho e aparelhamento ou ajuda ao transporte.

Ordenamento de posto de trabalho

Sempre determinada a melhorar a minha saúde, em setembro de 2012, deposito um processo de ordenamento de posto de trabalho junto do meu empregador. O percurso do combatente começa então para longas e penosas solicitações. O primeiro obstáculo consiste na dificuldade para encontrar material adaptado à minha patologia. O segundo é fazer coincidir o material equivalente, por três fornecedores diferentes, à mesma tarifa. O terceiro é propôr um período de ensaio geralmente recusado pelos fornecedores. O quarto é recuperar orçamentos coerentes e justos por Internet em prazos razoáveis. A poltrona e o reinstalação-pé, emprestados graciosamente durante uma semana, foram-me entregues, em setembro de 2013, ou seja um ano após o meu pedido inicial seguidamente um escritório e um meioarmário. Em setembro de 2014, pedi ao meu empregador um estudo exaustivo ergonome de trabalho que poderia refinar o meu quadro de trabalho, perceber as minhas dificuldades, avaliar-o e compensar-o pela preconização de pequeno material. A oportunidade da compra de umarmário à pequenas gavetas com uma classificação ao comprido (tipo arquiteto) antes que a utilização atual de gordos arquivos de formato A4 à costass largo num grande armário parece-me judiciosa, da mesma maneira que um pequeno rato, das luvas chauffants e uma reinstalação-pulso.

O direito à compensação

O projeto de vida da pessoa constitui o direito à compensação da sua deficiência.

A prestação da deficiência financiada pelas coletividades territoriais do fornecimento de um armário mural à gavetas na cozinha bem como pequenos materiais de cozinha à pilhas como abre-caixa, abre-frasco, abre-garrafa, moinho de pimenta e de sal, descasca-legume e raspadeira.

Além disso, o ordenamento da minha sala de água foi financiado pelo meu arrendador com retirada de um chuveiro tamanco dos anos 70 para um chuveiro à barca plana de noventa cm bem como pela instalação de torneira à bocal longo aos diferentes pontos de água na cozinha e a sala de água.

Invalidez

A nível do CPAM, três categorias de invalidez ao trabalho existem sequência um acórdão em longa doença.

8 - Ajudas diversas

Ajuda humana

As mútuas atribuem ajuda humanas à domicílio (família, corrida, guarda de criança) para um período curto ou mesmo ao ano. Ao meu pedido, a minha mútua atribuiu-me uma ajuda doméstica excepcional durante vários anos. Pude contar sobre um apoio regular que economizava a minha energia e sobretudo permitia uma higiene do meu interior e acessoriamente uma ajuda à cozinha. Paralelamente, encomendei as minhas corridas por Internet num supermercado perto da minha habitação, com entrega à domicílio, na minha cozinha. Era prémices da entrega à domicílio, bem antes do "drive" criados por grandes insígnias comerciais para a encomenda por Internet e a entrega das corridas na mala mesmo do seu automóvel, à loja. Qual alívio!

A segurança social participa à esta prestação à saída de hospital.

A assistente social do pessoal ajuda os assalariados a montar processos e a propôr qualquer pedido de ajuda.

O serviço da dor dos hospitais alvo dos intervenientes especializados no seu alívio (acupunctura, massagens...) e oferta a oportunidade de tratamento num mesmo lugar.

Os momentos de solidão são grandes. Poderia comparar-o à saída da maternidade onde a mãe é esgotada de uma maternidade e um parto recente e que tem necessidade de apoio, de ajuda doméstica e culinária e de guarda temporária, alguém fiável sobre que apoiar-se. Um golpe de fio, uma visita de amizade, uma noite pizza, um cesto de frutos, um prato quente, uma saída ciné organizado, uma tarde hammam, um baby-sitter, um transferido ao mar para tomar uma taça de ar, etc.

Todo mas não piedade! Este sentimento que acentua mal e a tomada em conta do nosso ambiente da gravidade e o perigo. O papel do ambiente é por conseguinte essencial a fim de sair da isolamento.

Ajuda material e financeira

O ordenamento de posto talvez facilitado pelo seu empregador através do fundo para a inserção das pessoas deficientes na função pública e o sector privado.

O ordenamento da habitação por meio da prestação de compensação da deficiência (PCH) na Casa departamental das pessoas deficientes (MDPH) após ter depositado um processo reconhecimento de trabalhador deficiente.

O AGEFIPH abre o emprego às pessoas deficientes na construção de um projeto profissional, formação, adaptação ao emprego...

O empregador, na sua vertente social, traz uma ajuda financeira aos seus empregados para uma ajuda humana, e uma ajuda material.

A segurança social pode atribuir uma ajuda financeira sobre os cuidados dispendiosos, da mesma maneira que a mútua.

A cura termal é uma vantagem para obter mais conforto. Em Ald (afeição longa durada), a cura é reembolsada. Raras são as pessoas que não são aliviadas parcialmente mesmo. A sobrecomplementar oferta das prestações de reembolso a não negligenciarem. A sua subscrição é anual e pode ser utilizada um ou vários anos se necessidade.

O pedido de afeição longo durado é feito pelo médico para o percurso de saúde e os medicamentos ligados à afeição cuja tomada pelo CPAM permite o reembolso à cem para - cem.

Uma associação de ajuda ao fibromyalgiques foi criada. A tela é rico de informações úteis para as pessoas interessadas.

Terceira parte

O voo phénix

Sentia efetivamente que tinha ainda algo a aprender sobre a minha doença. Não me demitia a aceitar-o. A minha vontade de seguir em frente e de enfrentar-o, para diminuir-o e reduzir-o à nada era mais forte que .a.toda. Não! Não sou doente. Mim não se oporá.

1.

A caminho para uma vida melhor

Em setembro de 2013, a minha energia de conquistar a minha doença é sempre de actualidade. Giro-me para uma terapeutada fala a fim de melhorar a minha abertura oral e a flexibilidade da minha pele sobre o meu rosto. Ao telefone, para uma tomada de encontros, a terapeutada fala indica-me que não tenho necessidade de ela porque o meu elocução é audível. Propõe-me -me que gire para stomatologue que trata a boca e as detecções neurológicas.

Por possibilidade, aconselha-me stomatologue à oito quilómetros do meu lugar de habitação. Tem longa uma formação inicial. A sua missão é a ciência médica da cavidade oral.

A minha primeira tomada de contacto telefónica com a sua assistente dental deixou-me pasmado porque a consulta era ligada à uma rádio panorâmico oral para que o doutor pudesse ver com exatidão a origem dos meus mais. Era persuadida que não tinha nada aos dentes. Ia no dentista desde qualquer jovem e fazia-me tratar dos meus dentes regularmente. Demitia-me fazê-lo todo do mesmo modo o necessário porque a minha curiosidade e a minha vontade de avançar empurrava-me na ação.

Reencontro-me por conseguinte por ocasião do meu primeiro encontro em outubro de 2013, em fim de tarde, mim avanço-me num bairro calmo. A assistente, uma jovem mulher loura de uma quarentena de ano aos cabelos longos vestido de uma calças brancos aumentados de uma blusa branca e calçada de tamancos introduz-me na sala de espera branca na qual sou a única paciente. Tem o olhar vivo e impõe seu único prestance um "knowhow". Agradável e à escuta, explica-me a justificação da rádio panorâmico. Espero-me à cerca de surpresas mas certamente não as imaginada.

Seguidamente único, observo intrigado os quadros pendurados ao muro. Sou atraída em primeiro lugar por um grande quadro horizontal "Ressonâncias dentais" do Dr. Albert Roths sobre que figura uma fotografia panorâmico da maxila com a correspondência dos dentes numerados com o corpo e a sua repercussão sobre a saúde. Intrigado por este quadro que trono em fundo de sala de espera, leio e tento decifrar a significado em relatório com a minha dentição. Difícil análise que deixa-me ao mesmo tempo perplexo e curiosa de compreensão porque cada dente pode ser ao mesmo tempo responsável de sintomas corporais e pode dar também uma indicação sobre uma problemática psicológica do doente. Por exemplo, o dente n° 35 corresponde ao algodystrophie do ombro e a força muscular.

Outro quadro intitulado Fibromyalgique "à investigação dos seus eixos" explica o disfuncionamento dos eixos do corpo humano sobre um fibromyalgique em paralelo com a postura normal. Lista imponente que sentem, dos quais têm-se pena de, que deprime-o e que obstrui-o causa-me dos estremecimentos na costas.

Atento à estas indicações, não posso fazer uma relação real dado que para mim, por um lado, os meus dentes são sãos porque as visitas no dentista conectam-se desde os meus seis anos e por outro lado, o meu corpo é direito e suficientemente duro para não inclinar como sobre a imagem mural.

Ao longo dos anos, as cáries acumulavam-se, os gordos amálgamas e as coroas floresciam na minha boca no entanto mantida regularmente pelo meu dentista que, à cada um das minhas visitas, encontrava uma lugar para fazer girar o seu rodízio. Era por conseguinte que confia sobre o diagnóstico stomatologue que não podia acusar-me qualquer anomalia dental sobre os meus dentes. A minha boca era sã. Nenhum fazia defeito (exceto dois dentes de sabedoria arrancados os anos anteriores).

No entanto, estou à mil lugares de imaginar quem vai produzir-se e revolucionar a minha vida.

O doutor é stomatologue e osteopata dental, desde um cerca de trinta de anos. Curioso e em procura de explicações concretas e de formações para fazer evoluir o seu trabalho, interessou-se ao fibromyalgie desde várias décadas.

Acolhe-me uma grande sala de trabalho branca decorada de grande ficus perto da poltrona do doente e o seu grande escritório de madeiras em frente da porta de entrada. É grande e fino, aos cabelos grisalhos, de uma cinquentena de anos. Dá-me uma boa impressão na sua blusa branca de cirurgião. Questiona-me sobre a razão da minha vinda e consulta o meu "scanner" completamente. Inicialmente, suspeita um problema nas minhas gengivas a nível das incisivas inferiores à vista de um pequeno quisto. Seguidamente pede-me descalçar-se e emprestar longo ao tapete vermelho retangular ao solo sobre duas ida e volta a fim de ver a minha diligência. Informa-me que a minha diligência é incerta e que a minha bacia não é direita. Propõe-me então me que acocore-se. Na frente da minha impossibilidade devida às minhas rigidezes musculares em qualquer desenvolvem-o os músculos de das coxas e barrigadas perna, os braços e das costas, faz-me inclinar adiante, pernas e braços tensos. À ajuda de um metro, mede o meu major tenso que se situa à vinte e sete centímetros do solo. Por último, pede-me que reduza-se de trás. Executo-me dobrando ligeiramente as pernas. Não somente, não posso reduzir-se, mas além disso não posso recuperar-me se cair porque as minhas mãos impedem-me receber-me ao comprido porque quase são espessadas com dedos duros e inflados, corados às articulações cuja impossibilidade de abrir-o totalmente e de fechar-o obceca-me todos os dias.

Observo o seu rosto e o da sua colaboradora cujo estupor deixa-se ler facilmente. Conheço as minhas dificuldades mas o facto de mostrar-o põe-me rapidamente mal à vontade, reconhecendo as minhas fraquezas e as minhas incapacidades, à minha idade. Explico-lhe ser encarcerado no meu corpo endurecido desde oito longos anos e ter tido a impressão de ter envelhecido de cinquenta anos em cerca de horas! Tenso, o meu corpo parece-me duro como um robô!

O doutor propõe-me que instale-me sobre a poltrona, observa e análise a minha boca, apalpa manualmente a parte traseira do meu pescoço a nível da raiz do crânio. Seguidamente, faz um teste a fim de medir a corrente galvânico na minha boca. Põe-me "à massa" tocando um amálgama com um utensílio. Sem estar a fechar a boca nem engulir, refaço os exercícios precedentes sobre o tapete. O meu degrau fica mais pesado, mais ancorada no solo, o meu balancim ante ganha vinte centímetros e com a sua ajuda, chego me a acocorar-se aos dois terços. É incrível! O que fez? Aquilo é digno de um mágico! O meu corpo não responde mais da mesma maneira. Ganha em flexibilidade. Revivo! É o dia e a noite em cerca de segundos. Tenho a impressão de ter tido uma operação plástica ao rosto e sentir-me ligeiro como uma pluma. O doutor informa-me que os efeitos são temporários no máximo de cerca de horas porque a corrente em boca misturada à saliva induzirá um efeito de rigidez provado. Com efeito, a rigidez reinstalou-se na noite, bloqueando o meu pescoço e os meus ombros adiante, num torno insuportável.

Mas saio crescido desta experiência porque tenho por último a esperança de um futuro melhor. Otimista e cheio de entusiasmo, começo a sonhar de mobilidade.

O doutor lança-se então em explicações simples e concretas. A minha boca é percorrida de corrente elétrica entre os diferentes dentes induz numerosos pelos amálgamas na minha boca precisando: "Diria-se "Chernobil"! "

Trata-se do electro galvanismo oral. Os diferentes metais sobre os dentes tratados no chumbo ou amálgama (compostos de mercúrio, de dinheiro, de paládio, de níquel, de cromo, de berílio, de cobalto, de gálio, de molibdênio, de irídio, de índio e de titânio) combinados à uma uma uma saliva condutora e uma presença de micro-organismos (estreptococos mutantes e monilíase albicans) favorecem o electro galvanismo.

 A minha boca por conseguinte é preenchida de mercúrio! Nada surpreendendo que a minha saúde deteriorou-se. O meu corpo não pode mais suportar estas doses importantes de corpos estrangeiros nefastos. O facto é que a verruma esquelética é flagrante, o peso do meu corpo adiante com apoios plantares e dentais assim alterados. É necessário e importante proceder à sua retirada o mais depressa possível, de maneira lento e precisa, de acordo com um protocolo concretizado por um orçamento validado pelas duas partes:

- dois à três sessões de osteopatia dental não reembolsadas pela segurança social a fim de favorecer a oclusão. Trata-se de corrigir se necessidade o encerramento da boca emboitement da maxila sem dificuldade.

- Seguidamente, a análise dos dentes mais atingidos corrente galvânico a fim do tratar.

Os cuidados serão longos e dispendiosos tanto quanto a minha boca comporta uma dezena de coroas e amálgamas antigos. Após os cuidados, o meu corpo permanecerá ainda encarregado de mercúrio que eliminar-se-á progressivamente a partir de meses ou mesmo um ano. É indispensável beber diariamente dois à três litros de água além das bebidas anexo (chá, café...). Peço-lhe explicações sobre o quadro de coincidência dos dentes com problemas físicos afixado na sua sala de espera. O médico informa-me que os dentes estão estreita relação com a fisiologia do corpo. Estão relação direto com um órgão ou vértebras; os músculos das maxilas e os da bacia estão conexão. Consequentemente, as tensões musculares não equilibradas dores lateralmente provocam às cavilhas, os joelhos, e os quadris. Precisa a necessidade de ter uma visão global do corpo e não um só um dente a tratar.

Além disso, o amálgama (ou chumbo) é obturation mais conhecido e mais utilizada constituído de uma mistura de diferentes metais cinquenta dos quais quase para - cem de mercúrio, trinta para - cem de dinheiro, trinta para - cem de cobre e estanho, bem como o zinco, o berílio, o zinco, do dinheiro ou o paládio...) para melhorar as qualidades obturation. As suas vantagens são múltiplas que vão da facilidade de manipulação, a rapidez de instalação, à grande resistência mecânica e a boa impermeabilidade sobre o longo termo bem como um custo fraco com reembolso pela segurança social na França.

Mas à extremidade de cerca de anos, os efeitos negativos sobre a saúde provocam a liberação de cerca de cinquenta para - cem do mercúrio na boca ou os órgãos do corpo (cérebro, rim, fígado, sistema gastrintestinal). Este disfuncionamento é acentuado pelo electrogalvanismo que põe em presença dois metais diferentes em boca com um líquido (amálgama e coroa ou prótese e saliva). Infecções bacterianas e virais ou ainda dérèglement do sistema imune com o aparecimento de doenças autoimunes ataca qualquer corpo são. Único dépose dos amálgamas de acordo com um protocolo adequado não prejudicial ao doente é indispensável para não acentuar os efeitos nefastos sobre o corpo humano. Poucos práticos lançam-se na aventura. Foi fiel ao meu dentista durante trinta e cinco anos, até seu a partida em reforma. Nunca ousou tentar a experiência, pretextando os prejuízos da intervenção ao lucro da sua manutenção em boca tendo em conta a sua antiguidade.

A consulta terminada, tomo consciência com ceticismo que o meu encontro é crucial e que é o ponto de partida para uma nova vida misturando ao mesmo tempo numerosas interrogações de confiança que tenho desejo de dar à este desconhecido. Mas a experiência tenta-me tendo em conta o resultado convincente desta primeira consulta.

De regresso ao meu domicílio, refleti ao discurso apoiado pelo doutor. Interrogava-me ao mesmo tempo sobre a veracidade das suas declarações e sobre as suas competências. Se todo fosse verdadeiro, a prática seria corrente e reconhecida do governo. Consultei o seu sítio muito explícito que me parece fazer claramente surgir as suas competências. Dá conferências, formações e escreveu mesmo um livro sobre o assunto.

Hesitei muito a investir-me neste processo. O desafio é importante: recuperar a minha saúde. Ponho na balança o número de anos onde as frustrações, as crispações, as tensões musculares e numerosas as impossibilidades diárias exasperam-me bem como a perda real de cerca de dez anos da minha vida neste constrangimento e sobretudo a sensação de ser velhas do duplo da minha idade! O orçamento a investir é incerto mas consequente dado que as melhorias constatar-se-ão progressivamente e a duração parece estender-se sobre o ano, ou mesmo mais. E dizer que pensava não ter nada a tratar na minha boca! Qual divulgação!

2.

Renascimento

O meu próximo encontro em novembro de 2013 é destinado de solucionar importantes os problemas de desequilíbrio occlusal de tipo ostéopathique. À ajuda do rodízio, trata-se de ajudar as minhas maxilas a fechar-se sem embaraço, e a liberar os seus movimentos laterais e antes de trás e de reequilibrar os apoios da minha maxila. As primeiras constatações são alarmantes. Ao encerramento da minha boca, tenho nenhum movimento possível adiante, de trás, nem sobre os lados. As minhas maxilas são encarceradas uma contra o outro sem possibilidade de movimento. Recordo-me ter alertado o meu dentista nos anos 1990 sobre esta sensação exatamente após ter realizado um gordo amálgama. A sua resposta esteve como um cutelo, recusando a minha constatação, com sem dúvida o sentimento de pôr na falta disso as suas competências.

Cerca de golpes de rodízio atrasado na sequência de marcas orientadas, a minha maxila desfazem-se instantaneamente. Tenho então a sensação agradável a ser liberada. Ao mesmo momento, uma onda emerge nas minhas barrigadas perna, como uma torrente viva que circula nas minhas pernas e os meus pés. Retomo possessão do meu corpo.

É suficiente imaginar a felicidade, o bem ser, a esperança reencontrada e o conforto sobre a única utilização do rodízio! Sinto-me de uma ligeireza que mim faltava desde assim muito tempo. Duas sessões de trinta minutos cada uma foi suficiente para vir à extremidade destes desagrados.

O mês seguinte, em dezembro, vem o encontro em stomatologue que transformou a minha vida de maneira fenomenal, inesperada e mágico porque o primeiro encontro deu o tom para o renascimento, a minha ressurreição e a esperança para uma vida melhor.

1 - Medidas da corrente galvânico

O doutor mediu a taxa de corrente galvânico cada uma dos meus dentes. A medida aceitável é menos de 100 milivolts (mV) e menos 10 micro-ampères (meu) por dente. Mas a minha boca apresentava este dia dos dados calculados incríveis.

Os dentes são numerados assim, da direita para a esquerda sobre a maxilar: dente de sabedoria 18 - molares (17 - 16) - prémolaires (15 - 14) - canino 13 - incisivos (12 - 11 - 21 - 22) – canino 23 - prémolaires (24 - 25) – molares (26 - 27) - dente de sabedoria 28 e sobre a mandíbula: dente de sabedoria 48 - molares (47 - 46) - prémolaires (45 - 44) – canino 43 – incisivos (42 - 41 - 31 - 32) - canino 33 - prémolaires (34 - 35) – molares (36 - 37) - dente de sabedoria 38.

Maxilar: prémolaires: n° 15: 81 mV - n° 24: 143 mV- n° 25: 142 mV e molares: n° 16: 89 mV e n° 17: 76 mV - n° 26: 107 mV

Mandíbula: prémolaires: n° 35: 196 mV - n° 45: 200 mV - molares: n° 36: 131 mV - n° 37: 125 - n° 46: 215 mV - n° 47: 89 mV - dente de sabedoria n° 38: 152 mV

2 - Origens prováveis do fibromyalgie

Tinha feito investigações sérias sobre a evolução dos sintomas, a inflamação muscular e as relações com os cuidados dentais e o meu percurso médico através de um quadro detalhado.

Olho como uma evidência o andamento passado até ao fibromyalgie: a tomada tétracycline à idade de três anos, a minha gravidez, as minhas duas coroas postas à seis e nove meses após o nascimento da minha rapariga, gordos os problemas intestinais justo após a refeição que seguiram, seguidamente a minha inflamação muscular apenas cinco meses após a instalação da última coroa e três meses após a vacinação do DT paralisia infantil.

Prova-se que após o nascimento da minha rapariga em outubro de 2004, consultei um dentista de qualquer urgência (não podia-lhos receber-me) sete meses após para mais de dente em maio de 2005 que pôs uma coroa de cerâmica sobre o molar n° 46 após uma hora de trabalho. Tenho a lembrança que tinha do mal a trabalhar, sobretudo sobre os canais da minha raiz muito enervando-se. Seguidamente, dois meses após, em julho, uma outra visita um outro em dentista de substituição terminou-se por outra coroa de cerâmica sobre o prémolaire n° 35. Em setembro do mesmo ano, faço-me vacinar pelo meu não especialista do DTP. Quatro meses atrasado, sofro de inflamação muscular generalizada. As coincidências são impressionantes à cerca de meses de intervalo, qual que a priori, sem relação de causa à efeito até meu a consulta deste famoso mês de dezembro.

3 - Dépose dos amálgamas

Stomatologue decide começar a retirada da coroa sobre o molar n° 46 - posto inicialmente desde oito anos e metade, em maio de 2005 seguidamente substituído por uma mútua dental em 2008 (apenas três anos após) - cuja intensidade é muito elevada em milivolts. Após ter utilizado o rodízio para recortar-o, extrai-o da minha boca e a instalação sobre o meu torso. O meu pescoço comporta rigidezes das quais os dois pontos de pressão ligados ao fibromyalgie permanecem duros e dolorosos. Os meus braços são duros quando o doutor tenta posicionar-me -o um após outro de trás a minha cabeça. Dores musculares puxam-me e impedem-me levantar-o de trás a minha cabeça. Seguidamente, deposita-o com a sua pinça sobre a prateleira de trabalho, à cinquenta centímetros do meu corpo. Pratica novos testes sobre o meu pescoço que se abranda instantaneamente. Os meus braços passam de trás a minha cabeça sem dificuldade. Ao mesmo momento, sinto então nas minhas pernas um fenómeno estranho. A circulação faz-se naturalmente, tal uma torrente que vaza nas minhas barrigadas perna e até meus a pés durante toda a duração da intervenção. Tenho a impressão de uma ligeireza. Pede-me então levantar-se e andar ao longo do seu tapete vermelho para ver o fenómeno. Após um momento de perda de marcador físico, o meu corpo domina-se e o meu degrau fica mais certo, os pés ancorados bem no solo. O doutor pede-me que reduza-me adiante pernas tensas. Executo-me. Enquanto que os meus majores tensos eram à vinte e sete centímetros do solo desde oito anos, reencontram-se sem nenhuma dificuldade à sete centímetros do solo. Não há! Os músculos os os da meus costas, as as minhas coxas, as minhas barrigadas perna, o meu pescoço e os meus braços autorizam-me por último reduzir-me adiante. Constato enquanto que o meu problema físico vem por conseguinte bem dos meus dentes. Nenhuma outra explicação é possível. Reganho a poltrona médica e o doutor descansa a coroa sobre o meu torso. O meu pescoço e os meus braços endurecem-se e as minhas mãos contratam-se. Efetua a tomada de marca e põe um dente provisório e dá-me encontros para outra sessão. Sou preenchida de felicidade. Não sou por conseguinte doente! A minha saúde vai por conseguinte melhorar-se de dia em dia como indicou-me -o.

Oito longos anos de vida monacal, privações, impedimentos físicos, baixa de moral, apreensão... Oito anos que impediram viver normalmente com a minha criança inferior idade e aproveitar plenamente, com a impossibilidade de levá-lo nos meus braços, levantá-lo, correr com ou reduzir-me, fazer degraus prolongados sem tensões musculares sobre as barrigadas perna, os ombros e o pescoço, jogar aos mapas ou qualquer jogo de manipulação, pôr joias, etc. Oito anos débrouillardise para conduzir-me ou lavar, para fazer a cozinha e os ato domésticos, para fazer a minha cama e efetuar tratar e tanto de outras dificuldades. A lágrima ao olho, ponho-me sonhar de um mundo melhor. Ouso esperar à melhoria da minha vida, o meu diário e o meu futuro que se anuncia brilhante. Este dia toca o renascimento, a minha vingança sobre a vida ainda que devo ainda pacientar um ano ou dezoito meses ou mesmo mais ainda para que elimine o mal que corrmói o meu corpo sem estar a gritar estação, que se propagou insensivelmente nos meus órgãos para reduzir-me à vida prisional, encarcerada no meu corpo mortificado. Revivo

O doutor pôs-me a coroa quinze dias após autocarro este lapso de tempos é indispensável para que o corpo habitue-se petit-à-petit e evitar assim os desagrados físicos causados pela precipitação dos cuidados. Ora, quatro dias foram suficientes de modo que quebrasse-se na minha boca à pressão do alimento. Prova-se que tenho uma alergia importante à zircônia e que posso ter apenas coroas especiais "lavei ultimate" e não "inlay core". O teste foi realizado pelo doutor no seu gabinete aquando da minha consulta e o meu corpo tem reagido instantaneamente na crispação acentuada (pescoço, braços e mãos) com a coroa incriminada. Em possessão da minha nova coroa, a abertura da minha boca faz-se mais grande. Os meus colegas de trabalho fizeram-me de observar à este período uma nítida melhoria do meu rosto descansado e distendido com efeito de boa mina. Número entre pediram-me o meu segredo de beleza! A minha pele era revitalizada, alimentada, alegre, rosada e aliviada, distendida com menos enrugar orais. Além disso, tendo em conta a circulação melhorada no meu corpo, eliminei os sobvestuários quentes polares desde este período e as camadas sobrepostas de vestuários na parte superior do corpo (sobpulôver, faixa ou lenço, boné). O meu estatuto de mulher extremamente timorata viu-se transformado.

Em março de 2014, novas medidas relativas à corrente galvânico são tomadas sobre as quais a corrente reduziu-se sensivelmente no conjunto após a retirada dos mais importantes dosados três meses anteriormente:

Maxilar: prémolaires: n° 15: 78 mV - n° 24: 103 mV- n° 25: 63 mV e molares: n° 16: 85 mV e n° 17: 66 mV - n° 26: 93 Mv

Mandíbula: molares: n° 36: 100 mV - n° 37: 101 - n° 47: 89 mV A constatação da diminuição da dosagem mV é que apreende sobre os dentes restantes. São vinculadas entre pela corrente galvânico.

Retirada dos mais dosados influencia inevitavelmente à baixa os números.

O molar nº 37 é preenchido de amálgama dental. Dépose do mercúrio sob dique dental é indispensável. Trata-se de um quadrado de látex muito fino e flexível totalmente impermeável que visa à proteção qualquer intrusão do mercúrio por via oral nos órgãos vitais.

Ao fim de abril, chega seguidamente o arranque do meu dente de sabedoria nº 38 que não tem pingente sobre a maxila oposta que pode causar perturbações corporais. Foi tratada repetidamente e comportada um gordo amálgama no seu centro e um pequeno sobre uma das espinhas.

O arranque foi longo e cicatrisation deu-me dores durante uma quinzena de dias.

Posso afirmar que à primavera 2014, nítidas melhorias físicas fazem-me reencontrar a minha energia e o meu dinamismo. Vi igualmente um forte alívio dos nódulos sobre as minhas articulações. Os meus braços são mais móveis e podem doravante funcionar mais facilmente de trás ou no ar. Reencontro sensações agradáveis de movimentos. Sequência ao abrandamento das tensões e inflações, os meus antebraços reencontram flexibilidade. A sensação de extremidade de madeiras desapareceu.

Com dépose da coroa nº 35 em junho de 2014 (posto inicialmente em junho de 2005 dos quais a intensidade é muito elevada em milivolts), ainda uma revolução no meu corpo faz-se sentir. Pude constatar fenómenos importantes de melhoria como a abertura oral mais grande à quatro centímetros e metade em vez de dois centímetros dez milímetros (com lucro de dois centímetros quatro milímetros), um forte alívio dos nódulos sobre as minhas articulações (cotovelos, joelhos) e desaparecimento a nível as cavilhas, das minhas baixofaces tornados a encher, uma flexibilidade e uma coloração da minha pele com alívio da seca a nível das mãos e processo de deflação comprometido dos tendões dos dedos, uma melhor mobilidade em étirement possível dos pés e dedos do pé e as noites corretas de oito horas de sono. Tenho uma sensação de viver na flexibilidade ainda que é ainda duro. Faço a relação evidente da ressonância dental sobre o corpo: a força muscular retorna gradualmente graças à este dente (quadro de Dr. Roths) como se um esclarecimento era a caminho.

Seguidamente, dépose dos amálgamas continua durante o verão, a coroa n° 45 e o gordo amálgama sobre o dente n° 47 melhoram gradualmente o conjunto das minhas perturbações.

Em julho, com o dente n° 45 (igualmente fortemente dosado em milivolts): dépose da coroa e reconstituição da espiga titânio T core, as minhas baixofaces ganham ainda em volume. Modelado do rosto retoma uma forma conveniente.

Desde o verão 2014, reencontra a possibilidade de datilografar nas mãos. Entendo o barulho golpear-o das minhas mãos uma contra o outro com força, e ao comprido. Posso além disso, graças à deflação dos tendões das falanges perto da palma das mãos, cruzar os meus dedos. Oito longos anos durante os quais era-me impossível cruzar os meus dedos! Aquilo parece insensato mas no entanto este gesto não fazia mais partir do meu diário. O único facto de pensar faz-me frio na costas!

Em setembro e outubro de 2014, as coroas sobre os prémolaires 24 e o 25 são depositados seguidamente substituídos.

À aurora do ano 2015, sucedem-se as intervenções com retiradas dos gordos amálgamas dos molares 15 e 16 seguidamente à primavera do 26 e 27. A cor acinzentado atenuou-se sobre os meus dentes (caninos) que ficaram mais brancos.

Mais dolorosa foi o 27 porque encontra-se basicamente da boca. Os meus lábios não suportavam mais a abertura prolongada e desenvolvem-o os músculos de queimavam-me ao canto dos lábios.

O doutor tinha imensamente mal a trabalhar porque quase progredia ao cego. Era alongada ao horizontal sobre a sua poltrona e ele posicionado través para chegar a finalizar o seu trabalho que durou uma hora durante

É grato do profissionalismo stomatologue, competente e apaixonado pelo seu de trabalho que procura aliviar o doente apesar de grandes dificuldades de acordo com os seus doentes. Devo-me tornar-lhe homenagem e agradecê-lo bem cordialmente ao seu justo valor. Trabalha desde um cerca de trinta de anos de modo que os seus doentes conheçam o benefício dos seus diagnósticos e as suas competências no quadro o seu trabalho. Fiz um encontro capital na minha vida e desejo transmitir a minha experiência enriquecedora que pode procurar um tal bem-estar que seria egoísta não difundir a informação à todos.

Seguidamente, uma coroa aço (molar n° 36) fica sempre em boca. Ora, três sessões de ajustamentos foram necessárias em cinco meses. O doutor tomou a decisão de substituir-o à ocasião porque parecia-lhe que não era anódino. À verdade dizer, sentia-me como embrumée, como "no vaps", esvaziado, sem vivacidade, constrangimento de avançar sem estar a ver a extremidade, sobrecarregado mais menor pelo trabalho, à extremidade antes de começar, sem energia e sem poder. Progressivamente das semanas, sentia um embaraço que se amplificava em boca. À cada mastigação, os alimentos encontravam-se cativos e pendurados entre dois dentes. O lado oposto tinha os mesmos sintomas. Passava a ser difícil comer facilmente. Devia tomar uma cura-dente para sair os alimentos dos seus alojamentos.

Em dezembro, a surpresa foi grande aquando da sua retirada. O mercúrio abrangia o meu dente desvitalizado! O procedimento específico foi adotado sob dique. Após os cuidados, um dente provisório foi posto.

Saí do seu gabinete com uma vitalidade, uma energia e um desejo de fazer um cem metros! Surpreendo-me sempre dos sintomas benéficos após a minha passagem em stomatologue. Qual felicidade de sentir-se ligeiro! Qual sentimento de liberdade!

Sempre sou surpreendida dos benefícios instantâneos recebidos à cada cuidado. Redescubro à cada sessão a surpresa de sentir sensações importantes dentro do meu corpo e sobretudo esta onda nas pernas. Chego a saber qual lugar o embaraço está na boca para um pequeno ajustamento. Sinto as dores musculares evoluir. Estou tanto à escuta que desenvolvi esta competência. Sou com efeito uma das raras pessoas que seja hipersensível.

Qual prazer de dirigir-me mais facilmente! Qual alegria de progredir e ganhar sempre em mais flexibilidade! Saí da sessão cheia de energia. Entreguei-me à escrita do meu livro a noite mesma empurrado por uma força sobrenatural, um desejo de avançar e finalizar o meu objetivo fixado e de concretizar o fim do meu percurso sobre a tela.

3.

Todas as asas estendidas

Treze dentes desprovidos de mercúrio e mistura nocivos para o meu corpo humano voltaram a dar um golpe de fenda ao esmalte dental. Não tenho mais em boca mercúrio doravante. No entanto, o meu corpo sofre ainda os prejuízos desta intoxicação, deste envenenamento nos meus órgãos.

De dia em dia, ganho também em flexibilidade, a minha pele rosada sofre cada vez menos de seca, reencontro sensações esquecidas desde há quase uma década: secar uma esponja, reduzir-me, me acocorar-se, aplaudir, cruzar os dedos... e posições mesmo fazer cerca de ioga. A minha força muscular retorna gradualmente ainda que sou ainda de cinquenta para - cem das capacidades musculares de uma mulher da minha idade. Faço um rápido ponto sobre a regressão do fibromyalgie e constato com estupefação que não tenho mais colite, ballonnement, de rhinite. Únicos cerca de pequenos nódulos isolados são aparentes sobre o cotovelo esquerdo e o joelho direito. Opõem-se ainda contractures às mãos e as pernas e a pequena tosse matinal ocasionalmente.

Stomatologue trouxe-me verdadeira uma emissão corporal. Ganhei setenta para - cem de benefício físico. Voltou-me a dar o gosto de viver, mover, o desejo de viajar, viver a tempo inteiro, de compartilhar saídas com a minha rapariga, de arejar-me, fazer projetos e de realizar-o, dar da cor à minha vida.

Da cinquentena de sintomas do fibromyalgie do qual sofria desde oito longos anos, sou doravante de apenas uma pequena dezena em dois anos de cuidados dentais. Posso apenas constatar a perigosidade do mercúrio para estar humano em proporções importantes e prejudiciais. Já tenho ganho pelo menos vinte anos.

Contaria continuar a inverter o processo nos meses vir. O tempo vai ainda ajudar à minha melhoria para uma flexibilidade sempre mais importante graças evacuação à progressiva mercúrio nos meus órgãos em qualquer meu corpo.

Meu considerar de vida resume-se neste simples provérbio: "Fazer contra qualquer má fortuna, bom coração" porque em frente de um destino desfavorável, aceitar que não se pode recusar, com de coragem qual único custa e procurar tirar melhor lucro.

Quarta parte

O fibromyalgie

e as despesas de saúde

1.

Diagnóstico do fibromyalgie
ou doença do cansaço crónico

O colégio americano de reumatologia posicionou em 1990 dezoito pontos de pressão sobre o corpo (com base no crânio e o pescoço, as articulações entre a segunda costa e o esterno, os bordos do músculo trapézio, os bordos internos das omoplatas, as partes superiores das nádegas, os cotovelos, quadris e o interior dos joelhos. O diagnóstico de fibromyalgie pode ser posto à oitenta e oito para - cem se onze entre eles forem dolorosa e tensa.

No entanto muito tempo considerada como uma doença psiquiátrica, o fibromyalgie é reconhecido desde 1992 pela Organização mundial da Saúde (OMS) como uma doença reumático.

O fibromyalgie (fibro: ligamentos, tendões – myo: músculos – dor: dor) é uma doença que evolui e se reflete no corpo humano num número importante de sintomas (perto de uma centena) da qual a principal é a baixa dos desempenhos físicos (fatigabilité muscular, os acouphènes, as alergias, perturbação do trânsito intestinal, perturbações visuais, ORL, o do sono e do humor, as rigidezes matinais, o cansaço geral crónico...), a baixa dos desempenhos intelectuais e a sensibilidade ao calor e as mudanças de temperatura. Acrescentam-se das dores e muitas das contractures que desequilibram o eixo do corpo e acentuam este fenómeno. Para certas pessoas, as dores movem sobre o corpo, quando para outros a enxaqueca, o cansaço crónico ou as contrações musculares instalam-se.

Às zonas mais dolorosas são geralmente próximas da coluna vertebral, a parte superior do corpo (a nuca, os ombros, a zona compreendida entre os dois ombros, as omoplatas) e a cintura da bacia (partes inferiores das costas, os quadris). Milhões de pessoas sofrem no mundo e não sabem para que girar-se para diminuir e sobretudo parar este déchaînement de desequilíbrios físicos. Infelizmente, nenhum captor biológico determina a origem destes mais.

O fibromyalgie compreende três fases: a vida diária é afetada parcialmente, a patologia instala-se de maneira crónica com dores intensas noturnas e diários e perturba as relações sócios profissional, e o paciente isola-se.

O seu desencadeamento é geralmente ligado à períodos intensos de vividos psicológicos doloroso ou ainda intolerâncias alimentares ou os metais pesados.

Em França, três à cinco para - cem da população são tocados, três dos quais quarto é geralmente mulheres e ao redor da quarentena.

É suficiente no entanto visualizar o corpo humano assim mortificado e fazer as primeiras constatações analisando o degrau do doente: ombro é mais um baixo que .o.outro e os quadris partem de um mesmo lado. O corpo não é mais no seu eixo e os apoios plantares posteriores são inexistentes. Assim, todo o peso do corpo é balançado para a frente do esqueleto. A costas, os ombros, o pescoço e os membros superiores e inferiores assim são solicitados de maneira inadequada e perdidos os seus marcadores, aumentando desequilíbrios e tensões.

A fim de identificar esta doença, é importante pôr-se as boas perguntas sobre a sua capacidade:

a) de um ponto de vista higiene da casa: fazer a cozinha, a louça à mão, as corridas, as camas, a lixívia em máquina, passar o aspirador;

b) de um ponto de vista social: ir ver amigos ou família, conduzir um automóvel, montar as escadas, fazer a jardinagem, andar várias centena de metros;

c) de um ponto de vista físico: ter dores, ser cansado, duras, inquietas, deprimido.

O diagnóstico do fibromyalgie é simples porque as respostas são geralmente positivas.

O fibromyalgie ou doença do cansaço crónico é a doença do século porque anestesia qualquer atividade do corpo humano. Torna cada ação física difícil ou mesmo impossível num estado de cansaço latente. Desenvolve-se para tocar cada vez mais inocentes vítimas. Numerosos questionários de avaliação foram postos em lugar bem como escalas de avaliação dos sintomas e a dor.

Uma lista posiciona cem sintomas do fibromyalgie. A dor pode concretizar-se sob forma de dores musculares, golpes de punhal, sensações de queimaduras ou de picaduras, de quitações elétricas, de formigamentos e a impressão de entorpecimentos musculares.

2.

Cargas financeiras

As pessoas que sofrem de fibromyalgie custam caro à sociedade.

1 - Cargas financeiras para a sociedade

As despesas comprometidas não especialistas, em especialistas e outras medicinas paralelas, acórdãos de trabalho, de tratamento e de exames médicos... representam mil milhões de euros ao título da população francesa. À escala de um ano, as publicações internacionais consideram à sete mil euros por pessoa as despesas comprometidos pelo ministério da saúde.

Esta estimativa está bem debaixo da realidade. O duplo seria mais adequado.

Devi fazer chamada ao corpo médico a fim de aliviar as minhas rigidezes e controlar o meu estado de saúde. Estive bem contra a minha vontade uma carga para a sociedade.

A declaração em afeição longa durada (ALD) provoca o reembolso integral das despesas comprometidas para a doença. As visitas médicas e cuidados são reembolsados: fisioterapia (1h30 por semana), allopathie e homeopatia (todos os meses), acupunctura (duas vezes por mês), dermatologia, reumatologia, cura de cuidados, ergoterapia com hospitalizações e exames médicos e bioquímicos e hematológicos, VSL, farmácia, ação social da segurança social, ajuda-doméstico, ou seja um total de14.000 euros arredondados por ano. Acrescentam-se o acórdão de trabalho de seis meses e o reembolso dos cuidados dentais (4000 euros). A carga total da segurança social e a mútua é por conseguinte de15.000 euros por ano durante dez anos.

Seguidamente o ordenamento de posto, do alojamento, a prestação de compensação da deficiência, a ação social empregador, um total de despesas que criam-se à16.000 euros é 1.600 euros por ano durante dez anos.

O custo global do Estado para a minha única pessoa durante dez anos é 166.000 euros.

Um complemento de despesas à carga do paciente para obter um conforto corporal: osteopatia, magnétiseur, complementos alimentares, balnéothérapie, produtos de beleza (natas para o corpo, o rosto e as mãos)... 1000 euros cerca de por ano e de kinésiologue e cuidados dentais até 9.000 euros ou seja à minha carga um orçamento gasto de 19.000 euros em dez anos.

É inevitável multiplicar a integralidade destas despesas pelo número de anos durante os quais a doença reinou.

Em dez anos, 185.000 euros foram gastos pela coletividade para aliviar as minhas perturbações de saúde.

2 – Financiamento

Estas gordas despesas excepcionais comprometidas para melhorar a minha saúde agravaram inevitavelmente o meu orçamento. Os meus projetos consequentemente reduziram-se à nada.

Os cuidados corporais são necessários para ter um mínimo conforto de vida num corpo de velhos. As minhas despesas dentais fizeram o objeto de reembolsos mínimos com base em coroas clássicas pela pela segurança social e minha mútua à concorrência de cem oitenta euros por dente, completados pelo meu seguro complementar até dois cem quarenta e sete euros por dente à concorrência de mil cinco cem euros para um ano.

No entanto, estas despesas não fazem o objeto nem de um capricho de ma part, nem uma necessidade estética mas bonita e bem uma necessidade vital para parar o envenenamento de mercúrio do qual fui vítima.

3.

E se o segredo encontrasse-se nos vossos dentes?

O fibromyalgie de origem dental é uma doença que não deveria existir. A gratuitidade deste mal ligada ao mercúrio em boca, prejudicial ao comum do mortais, é inadmissível para o paciente. O organismo é obriga de engulir quantidades nocivas de produtos tóxicos no entanto prejudiciais para o ambiente. Nenhum olhar benevolente interrompe esta cadeia nefasta e perigosa de utilização do mercúrio.

O Conselho superior de higiene pública da França (CSHPF) publicou um relatório em 1998 que dá informações e preconiza recomendações sobre a utilização dos amálgamas.

Na França, excelente o relatório de informação n° 261 (2000-2001) muito fornecido sobre "os efeitos dos metais pesados sobre o ambiente e a saúde" do Sr. Miquel faz em nome do Serviço parlamentar de avaliação das escolhas científicas técnicas (depositado o 5 de abril de 2001 ao Senado) revela na sua segunda parte de preciosas informações sobre o mercúrio no amálgama dental. Não foi seguido de factos concretos nem de medidas excepcionais de decisão governamentais. No entanto, a sua leitura é rico de ensinos e descobertas sobre o mercúrio e os seus prejuízos sobre a saúde.

1 - Os efeitos do amálgama

O seu parágrafo C precisa os efeitos do amálgama dental, material utilizado para obturar as cavidades de tecidos dentais afetados por cáries. Embora chamado também chumbo, não comporte chumbo. É constituído de mercúrio líquido (uma grama cerca de por amálgama) e outros metais de pó como o dinheiro, o cobre, o estanho, o zinco destinado a melhorar o tempo de tomada ou as propriedades mecânicas finais da mistura. A vantagem principal de esta mistura consiste sobretudo uma boa impermeabilidade. Acrescentam-se à aquilo uma perenidade no tempo, uma facilidade de manipulação e uma rapidez de instalação, e um custo relativamente fraco.

Os inconvenientes dos amálgamas deve-se do produto, os inestéticos e a técnica de posto específica, e sobretudo a toxicidade pela liberação do mercúrio e o electro galvanismo oral. O electro galvanismo cria-se por correntes elétricas, muito de baixa tensão que são geradas pela proximidade dos materiais metálicos heterogéneos. A cavidade oral constitui um puzzle organizado de materiais diferentes (amálgamas de diferente geração, misturas para próteses e implantes...), que geram poderes elétricos diversos. Permitem uma liberação de íons metálicos que conduzem à formação de uma corrente galvânico (corrente elétrica muito de baixa tensão, estudada por Galvani). Produz-se então uma liberação de íons metálicos quando um amálgama encontra-se perto de outros metais, em especial de uma mistura metálica mais eletropositiva, a saliva que joga então o papel de eletrólise. Assim, certos cientistas pensam que à extremidade de dez anos, com a saliva e a mastigação dos alimentos, os dois terços do mercúrio inicial são eliminados.

Ora um amálgama emite vapores dos quais uma parte é absorvida pelos pulmões. O mercúrio passa no sangue, atravessa a barreira hémato-encéphalique, então é prendido e acumulado no cérebro, principal órgão orienta. A mistura de vapores à corrosão da saliva, produto dos íons mercuriques, do qual uma parte parece atravessar a parede do intestino graniza e acumular-se em vários órgãos até a oxidação e transformação de sais de mercúrio para causar estragos.

Os compósitos para as pequenas cáries que não permitem obturation eficaz a longo prazo sem garantia de impermeabilidade, a instalação de amálgama é privilegiada. A sua multiplicação em boca é crítica dado que sabe-se que a instalação e dépose de amálgamas são dois momentos críticos que arriscam aumentar brutalmente os vapores de mercúrio da mesma maneira que o número de amálgamas em boca (limiar critica à sete). Um estudo canadiano preconiza quatro amálgamas para os adultos, três para os adolescentes, e um para as crianças.

O relatório de informação detalha os três tipos de consequências sobre a saúde:

a) as reações locais (alergias e o electro galvanismo);

b) as perturbações e doenças graves: A toxicidade do mercúrio é conhecida: As perturbações neurológicas, neuromusculaires ou cardiovasculares, nefríticos, os sobre a fase de crescimento intra-utérine, immun toxicidade (o impacto do mercúrio sobre as defesas imunes alterando a flora intestinal, o mercúrio provocaria uma sensibilidade acrescida às agressões externas e poderia tornar-o resistente aos antibióticos.)

c) e as consequências gerais.

2 - Grupos à riscos

Interessa-se igualmente aos grupos à riscos:

a) As mulheres grávidas: A partir de 1980, a OMS recomendava limitar a exposição das mulheres em idade de gerar. Na França, esta medida fez o objeto de uma dupla recomendação tanto do CSHPF do 19 de maio de 1998 como do Conselho de aproximadamente os cirurgião-dentistas. É judicioso observar que esta medida foi adotada apenas após um prazo de vinte anos.

b) As outras pessoas à riscos: jovens crianças (allaitement e mastigação de borrachas a mastigarem), os adultos enfraquecidos (alérgicos e sobretudo ao mercúrio ou sofrendo de insuficiência renal) e os adultos à multicáries.

c) Os práticos: Os médicos stomatologistes, cirurgião-dentistas, assistentes dentais são aos primeiros e mais expostos ao mercúrio do amálgama. A exposição tem lugar ao momento a da preparação, a instalação, dépose, a recuperação dos amálgamas, e o polimento do dente, oferecendo assim numerosas ocasiões de contacto direto e sobretudo inalação de vapores de mercúrio. O teor de mercúrio no ar dos gabinetes dentais de acordo com estudos europeus estica a justificar precauções e medidas elementares de higiene conhecidas recapituladas pelo CSHPF no seu parecer do 12 de maio de 1998.

3 - Mudança das mentalidades

Em 2007, o mercúrio foi classificados pela OMS como uma das dez substâncias mais tóxicas com o arsénico, o chumbo e o amianto.

Desde 2009, a OMS preconiza a eliminação progressiva dos produtos que utilizam mercúrio, incluindo os amálgamas dentais. Para tanto, a organização considera que uma proibição total a curto prazo "poria um problema para a saúde pública e o sector dental".

A posição oficial do nosso país é resumida no relatório da Agência francesa de segurança sanitária dos produtos de saúde (AFSSAPS) de outubro de 2005 que conclui à inocuidade amálgamas.

São no entanto proibidos nos países do norte da Europa: a Rússia (1975) e o Japão (1982), a Suécia (1999), a Noruega seguidamente a Dinamarca (2008). Vários outros países europeus a Áustria e a Alemanha seguiram o passo.

O mercúrio é reconhecido unanimemente hoje em dia como uma substância muito nociva para a saúde humana e o ambiente. Em especial é posto em causa na multiplicação "das doenças emergentes" (que se multiplicam desde os anos 1980): fibromyalgie, alergias, depressão, spasmophilie, enxaquecas, dores difusas, a doença de Parkinson, a esclerose em placas, o autismo... que poderiam também ser vinculado à uma intoxicação ao mercúrio.

O prazo entre a intoxicação latente ao seu início e o aparecimento dos sintomas pode ir até à quinze anos. O mercúrio difunde-se lentamente, duravelmente ao longo de toda a vida intraoral, viagem no nosso corpo sobre o conjunto dos nossos órgãos e grave e silenciosamente intoxica-aos portadores de amálgamas que absorvem sobre uma longa duração ínfimas umas quantidades de mercúrio.

De acordo com um relatório publicado em 2012 pela Comissão europeia, a França utiliza um terço das cinquenta e cinco toneladas de mercúrio cada ano na União europeia para a realização de amálgamas dentais. A convenção internacional de Minamata uma diminuição em outubro de 2013 prevê do uso dos amálgamas sem, no entanto, fixar de constrangimentos ou objetivos. A toxicidade do mercúrio nos amálgamas dentais continua a fazer debate.

4 - Questionnement

Como é possível incriminar na França ao mesmo tempo os amálgamas dentais, a sua retirada pelo um especialista (devidos aos vapores de mercúrio), e seu tratamento como desperdícios tóxicos (triagem num contentor especial), muito conservando-o em qualquer impunidade durante décadas em boca, encruzilhada dos órgãos vitais (cérebro, pulmão, intestino)?

O perigo sobre o ambiente seria mais prejudicial e mais digno de interesse para o governo que o seu impacto sobre o corpo humano?

É tempos de fazer alterar as mentalidades nomeadamente na França e todos os países europeus ou mesmo ao nível mundial que ainda não têm tomado a real medida dos estragos causados pelo mercúrio nos amálgamas dentais sobre o Humano. A utilização de um metal altamente tóxico para cuidados dentais, provavelmente à origem de uma intoxicação e doença autoimune é um escândalo sanitário.

Como pode-se então ainda surpreender-se da emergência de novas doenças e o desenvolvimento de certas doenças autoimunes? O princípio de precaução ou de prevenção não é utilizado para as pessoas atingidas da doença por muito tempo enquanto que o perigo do mercúrio é conhecido perfeitamente.

Não somente a pessoa sofre na sua carne ingurgitation de produtos nocivos em qualquer legalidade (antibiótico prescreve para jovens crianças para tratar de doenças infanteis enquanto que ele frágil os dentes apesar dos testes laboratório não suficientes e tétracycline é postos sobre o mercado sem contraindicação ou ainda o mercúrio nos amálgamas dentais), seguidamente da forte probabilidade do ocorrido de doença autoimune sem estar a gritar estaciona.

O sentimento de aprisionamento no sofrimento e o silêncio sobre a gratuitidade deste mal são particularmente insustentável para os pacientes.

A divergência de opiniões entre países faz frente à resistência europeia.

O Estado não deve mais ser um abismo para a sociedade que se compromete, través a segurança social, a aliviar e tratar de inocentes que não curarão nunca da nocividade mercúrio.

As medidas de proibição do mercúrio nos amálgamas são reservadas aos cerca de países muito minoritários na União europeia e poucos países globalmente no mundo que têm uma diligência responsável. , Pela sua ação, salvaram uma parte da sua população ao mesmo tempo sobre o plano da saúde humana, do ambiente e um ponto de vista financeiro.

Tomem exemplo sobre os nossos vizinhos que se comprometeram na responsabilização do bem-estar seus concitoyens. Garantam que andaremos nos seus passos nos anos próximos.

Continuem a sonhar à dias melhores onde o Humano esteja no meio da paisagem política.

Preservem a nossa bonita terra azul, qualquer em redondeza, protegida dos prejuízos do Homem, por medidas conservatórias concretas.

A nossa única vontade à escala mundial pode deixar às gerações futuras a marca ecológica indispensável ao nosso planeta.

Dão os meios a partir atualmente e falam de uma só uma voz: a nossa única força.

Conclusão

Desejei este livro em homenagem à todos os ser que sofrem na sua carne de fibromyalgie, que, pela sua coragem e sua imensa força de vida, vão poder certamente quebrar as relações que retêm-o prisioneiros e conectados ao passado. Dou-lhes a esperança de reencontrar a sua juventude demasiado rapidamente perdida.

Ofereço outro olhar sobre esta doença. Sair do aprisionamento do sofrimento não é não somente uma pergunta da vontade mas um objetivo a atingir. Soluções existem.

Espero ter aberto uma janela de esperança e de renascimento sobre o compromisso individual num combate diário para reaparecer tal phénix.

Agradecimentos

Desejo manifestar qualquer minha gratidão e o meu profundo respeito à esta mão tensa guiada pelo profissionalismo e as convicções do médico especialista stomatologue.

 Acompanhados da sua simpática colaboradora, souberam pontuar as sessões de notas de humor renovadas. Esquecerei nunca com qual precaução e paciência os cuidados foram prodigalizados na minha boca entre aberto pelas rigidezes e sobretudo este dia de outubro de 2013 onde a minha vida tomou outro que gira.

Tenho também um pensamento específico ao kinésiologue, a encruzilhada dos caminhos, que abriu as portas da criatividade, e ao ergoterapeuta que personalizou as suas sessões para o progresso positivo de lucros consequentes graças seus a competências profissionais e a sua empatia.

Tanto boa vontade para conduzir-me para um futuro melhor e prometedor, meus sonhados tornam-se por último "realidade".

＊

Agradeço igualmente cordialmente os meus pais: a minha mãe, que acreditou nmim e permitiu concretizar o meu projeto, e o meu pai cuja estrela brilha intensamente no meu coração e guia cada um dos meus passos.

MESA DAS MATÉRIAS

LISTA DOS LIVROS DO MESMO AUTOR

Adieu fibromyalgie ! Comment gagner 20 ans et retrouver une bonne santé em Francês - ISBN 979-10-95925-02-6
Parecido **em 2015**

Parecido **em 2016**

Good-Bye fibromyalgia ! How to gain twenty years and to find a good health em Inglês - ISBN 979-10-95925-17-0

Addio fibromialgia ! Come guadagnare 20 anni e trovare una buona salute em Italiano - ISBN 979-10-95925-20-0

Adiós fibromyalgie! Cómo ganar 20 años y encontrar una buena salud *em* Espanhóis - ISBN 979-10-95925-23-1

Lebewohl fibromyalgie ! Wie 20 Jahre zu gewinnen und eine gute Gesundheit wiederzufinden em Alemão - ISBN 979-10-95925-26-2

Adeus fibromyalgie ! Como ganhar 20 anos e reencontrar uma boa saúde em Português - ISBN 979-10-95925-53-8

Vaarwel fibromyalgie ! Hoe 20 jaar winnen en een goede gezondheid terugvinden em Neerlandês - ISBN 979-10-95925-50-7

*****

Petite étoile de Provence – Novela em Francês
ISBN 979-10-95925-02-6

Small star of Provence – Novela em Inglês - ISBN 979-10-95925-29-3

Piccola stella di Provenza – Novela em Italiano
ISBN 979-10-95925-35-4

Pequeña estrella de Provence – Novela em Espanhóis
ISBN 979-10-95925-38-5

Kleiner stem de Provence – Novela em Alemão
ISBN 979-10-95925-41-5

Pequena estrella de Provença - Novela em Português
ISBN 979-10-95925-44-6

Kleine ster van Provence - Novela em Neerlandês
ISBN 979-10-95925-47-7

*****

Au pays des Maharajahs - novela juventude **8/12** anos   em
Francês - ISBN 979-10-95925-13-2 6

With the country of the Maharajahs - novela juventude **8/12**
anos em Inglês - ISBN 979-10-95925-32-3

Al paese del Maharajahs – novela juventude **8/12** anos em
Italiano - ISBN 979-10-95925-56-9

Al país del Maharajahs - novela juventude **8/12** anos em
Espanhóis - ISBN 979-10-95925-59-0

*****

Sous l'Océan - Conto ilustrado para crianças **8/12** anos em
Francês - ISBN 979-10-95925-01-9

Ilustrações de cobertura: Fotolia – evgeniya_m

e Fotógrafo Alberto Gray - Châteauneuf-du-Pape

Documento impresso aos Estrados Unidos

por Amazon

Terminado imprimir em outubro de 2016

Depósito legal: em outubro de 2016

Les éditions Plum'issime

15 boulevard Limbert B- 84000 Avignon France

plumissime.fr   **plumissime123@gmail.com**

https://www.facebook.com/Laurence.Estienne.Auteur

N° ISBN 979-10-95925-53-8